Self-Made Me

Why Being Self-employed Beats Everyday Employment Every Time

Geoff Burch

CAPSTONE

This edition first published 2012

© 2012 Geoff Burch

Registered office
John Wiley & Sons Ltd, The Atrium, Southern Gate, Chichester, West Sussex,
PO19 8SQ, United Kingdom

For details of our global editorial offices, for customer services and for
information about how to apply for permission to reuse the copyright material in
this book please see our website at www.wiley.com.

Wiley publishes in a variety of print and electronic formats and by print-on-
demand. Some material included with standard print versions of this book may
not be included in e-books or in print-on-demand. If this book refers to media
such as a CD or DVD that is not included in the version you purchased, you may
download this material at http://booksupport.wiley.com. For more information
about Wiley products, visit www.wiley.com.

Designations used by companies to distinguish their products are often claimed as
trademarks. All brand names and product names used in this book are trade
names, service marks, trademarks or registered trademarks of their respective
owners. The publisher is not associated with any product or vendor mentioned in
this book. This publication is designed to provide accurate and authoritative
information in regard to the subject matter covered. It is sold on the
understanding that the publisher is not engaged in rendering professional services.
If professional advice or other expert assistance is required, the services of a
competent professional should be sought.

Library of Congress Cataloging-in-Publication Data
To follow

A catalogue record for this book is available from the British Library.

ISBN 9780857082657 (paperback) ISBN 9780857082756 (ebk)
ISBN 9780857082763 (ebk) ISBN 9780857082770 (ebk)

Set in 10/13.5 pt Sabon by Toppan Best-set Premedia Limited
Printed in Great Britain by TJ International Ltd. Padstow, Cornwall, UK

FOR DAVID AND ARCHIE
AND TO ALL THE BRAVE GO IT ALONERS WHOSE
TENACITY HAS INSPIRED ME TO WRITE THIS BOOK

It is said that in life you can either be a great example
or a terrible warning

CONTENTS

A NEW WAY OF LIVING IN A CHANGING WORLD

Welcome aboard the good ship Freedom! Maybe you have joined this happy adventure as a willing passenger. Perhaps this cheery vessel has heaved-to, to rescue you from the lifeboat of redundancy while your previous employer sinks without trace. Or maybe you have been rescued, having being marooned on the dreary island of unemployment. For whatever reason you have decided – or been forced – to accompany us, you have just joined the finest and most fulfilling way to cruise through life.

ARE YOU PAID WHAT YOU ARE WORTH?

Following that little ramble, I am now going to have to use the word, or words, that make me cringe and those are 'self-employment'. I desperately struggle to find a more suitable or politically correct alternative to the label that other people have decided to attach to those of us who work for ourselves. To make myself a bit clearer, let's take those phrases to bits and examine them. 'Self' – that's you or me; 'employed' – that's the job we have been given to earn our living. 'Work' – now there's an interesting word, and one that this book will look at a great deal, but for now, and without too much explanation, I suppose you could say 'work' is an activity that someone is prepared to pay you for. 'Ourself', of course, is you or me, which means that the revenue created by the 'work' belongs to you or me. Although that seems obvious, if you have a 'proper job' the revenue generated by your efforts will go to someone else, your employer. If you follow the advice and guidance in this book, you should be able to get paid what you are worth for your work whilst being self-employed. If your employer can get what you are worth for your work, it stands to reason that they will not give all the revenue to you – that is how they make a profit, by paying you less than you are worth.

PAID EMPLOYMENT – A NEW-FANGLED IDEA

Employment is a fairly new and short-lived idea that has probably had its day. You may feel that is a fairly outrageous comment, so let me explain.

If you go back a few hundred years, even the peasants were self-employed. The lord would give them free use of a piece of land and whatever profit the peasant made was tithed or shared with the lord by way of rent. While I am not suggesting a return to feudal agriculture, it is interesting to note that in mediaeval times no-one had invented the spine-chilling word, 'management'.

Stop here for a moment. Do you really want or need to be managed? Maybe as a 3- or a 15-year-old people would describe you as hard or easy to manage, but that was when your life was in other peoples' hands. However, now as a free adult, why on earth would you hand yourself over to be managed?

The feudal lord wasn't interested in managing anything. The peasants could get up when they wanted, plant what they wanted, and work when they wanted. What the lord was interested in was outcomes not process. If after a bumper harvest you filled the lord's tithing barn with crops, he wouldn't walk around with a stopwatch and clipboard saying, "How did you achieve this? Did you comply with the correct procedures and processes?"

The other big feature of self-employment is the incredible level of efficiency that it produces. In a previous book (*Go It Alone*), I examined the best way of getting people from one place to another as fast as possible by bicycle. The first method to consider would be to take, say, one hundred people and try and construct a single cycle that all one hundred people could ride on. The problem is that as the bicycle gets bigger, its efficiency starts to fall – even a tandem, which only carries two people, can have its problems because there will always be accusations between the two partners about who pedals the hardest. As the number of people grows, it becomes even more difficult to find out who is actually pedalling – and to support the weight of one hundred people, the bike would have to be massively heavy and ungainly to the point where, as it takes on extra pedallers, its weight increases and exceeds their ability to pedal. So picture the scene: you have this huge monster of a machine with a hundred people on it – some who don't bother to pedal at all, some who have to pedal furiously just to support their own weight, and then you have the problem of steering such an ungainly beast. Because of its bulk, the process of steering has to become a full-time job, so the people who steer it feel that they don't have to pedal as well because steering and choosing the direction of the bike is a full-time occupation.

This is like the modern company where the board of directors believes that they have to do nothing but steer, and the people that do the pedalling, the workers, feel that their steerers or directors make bad decisions and don't really work very hard. The other problem, of course, is that if any wrong decisions are made in steering or choice of direction and there is a crash, all one hundred pedallers are equally doomed.

So what is the correct way to do it? The self-employed equivalent is to give everybody their own bicycle. In a bicycle race, a group of racing cyclists is referred to as the peloton where they race against each other in a very efficient and swift manner. The one hundred people in the race – or at least most of them – will arrive at their destination at an astonishingly high average speed. Sure, a few will crash, but even most of those can hop back on and get started again without the drama of a one hundred-person machine crashing.

I thought about this analogy and have tried to tie it into the trouble and turmoil that we have seen in the world at the time of writing this book. I've realized that, rather than bicycles, perhaps a better way of looking at this would be to compare the world of work to a beehive. A beehive is not a business; the bees are not employees, they are a community. Each single bee leaves the hive and looks for wealth in the shape of pollen, which it carries back to the community. What would not work would be a four ton bee! There is no efficiency in size, it would be too big to bother with every little flower, it would be too big to cheerfully share its wealth and experience with other bees, and in truth it is probably too big to even get off the ground.

I am sure some employers will view this book as somewhat threatening and anti-social but in truth it is pro-social – all I am saying is that individuals who go and find their own value and wealth can contribute more efficiently and cheerfully to the community we live in.

I don't intend this book to be a book on how to start a 'business'. I have tried very hard to differentiate between the self-employed individual's way of making their way in the world, which I will refer to throughout this book as the 'enterprise', and the idea of starting a 'business', but I cannot avoid occasionally blurring the edges. It is possible that the self-employed individual may work with another, whether that is a partner or their spouse, or may occasionally employ another person in the shape of a trainee or an apprentice, but when does that become a business? I'm not sure but I think that is up to the reader to decide. Bizarrely, banks have a very strange view of this and will describe you as a 'business' the moment that you are not employed by somebody else – in fact, I fought long and hard with banks to try and get them to realize that there are actually three species of money earners, not two, i.e. businesses, employed, and self-employed, and just because you are self-employed it doesn't mean you run a business.

So, to sum up, although this book may stray into other territories, its real objective is to examine how the individual can achieve their true worth and value – both financially and emotionally – by employing themselves. After all, whoever you are, you will never find a boss to employ you who will value and treasure you as much as you will for yourself. My qualification for writing this book is that I have been self-employed for most of my working life, and for a lot of that time I have been professionally involved in helping small enterprises to succeed. Therefore, this book is based on my observations and experiences along the way. I have made most of the mistakes that I have highlighted and have also enjoyed a lot of the victories and benefits that are mentioned, so please read on and enjoy!

PART 1

THE CASE FOR SELF-EMPLOYMENT

CHAPTER 1

IT'S ALL ABOUT YOU

. . . In which we talk of steam engines, elephants and the nature of work. We also find out what we are worth to other people and ourselves and the best way of achieving our true value. Even a potato can move up in the world.

A HAPPY OUTCOME

One of the big mindset changes that the newly self-employed must realize is that we sell outcomes and we deliver outcomes. It is outcomes that our customers want and it is what they pay us for. Later in this book I state, "Consultancy is doomed." This provocative statement is made because I encounter so many ex-employed people who become 'consultants' and believe that they can be involved in a process that just goes on and on with no outcome, just the way their old job used to do. Customers (by the way, here is another word that requires definition – a customer is someone who will pay us to do the work; work is the activity the customer is prepared to pay us to do) want outcomes, or at least the promise of outcomes.

You, "I can fix that for you."

The customer may say "How?" but their real interest is "How much?"

They want their house painted, their lunch prepared, or their sales increased – we will negotiate a price to achieve those outcomes. We will be selling products or outcomes. The whole point of this book is to help you receive the maximum amount for achieving those outcomes. That amount is your value and when you get it it's all yours to keep.

TIED TO THE BIG MACHINE

So how did this employment thing start and how did all but the lucky self-employed become wage slaves? It's probably all about steam engines. Before these beasts, every machine tended to be human powered; one human, one machine, be it treadle lathe, loom or spinning wheel. Therefore, it stands to reason that the machine was where the person was and the person was where the machine was . . . which could be anywhere. I could sit at my treadle loom watching the sun sinking over the ocean whilst contemplating life and wondering what to have for supper. My income would be in relation to my work (remember, what I get paid for doing). This is very important because this could relate to speed, skill, ambition, age or inclination. It would have been me working the machine, not the machine working me. With a young, growing family I would go like the clappers, and then as they grew up and I became older. Why knock myself out? Maybe just a couple of hours a week.

This is really fascinating. Do you choose your own hours, and do you get more money if you are more efficient, or if you are less efficient can you ask for less money for reduced effort? As you age, can you slow down a bit? No? Then you aren't self-employed.

This is where the steam engine rears its ugly head. Some bright spark invented the steam engine which, after a bit of development, became so powerful it could drive many thousands of machines in one place. But here is the rub: the machines needed to be in one place, the place where the steam engine was. The whole place was driven by heavy spinning shafts that thundered on day and night at a constant speed. The thousands of machines needed thousands of operators, but they then had to leave their crofts and cottages to be where the steam engine was because it couldn't move. They had to work at the pace of the machine because it didn't change, and everybody had to work at the same speed for the same time because the engine dictated that. They got the same money and it was called a wage. If your speed was below that of the machine's, due to your age or ability, you would be fired (or retired). If your ability exceeded the machine, the mind-numbing boredom would crush that right out of you until you aligned with the machine.

The cruelty of training
Of course it has all changed now – or has it? We have appraisals and training that fit us to the engine and as we age and slow we are prepared for the chop. We do our job and we are judged by the process, not the outcome. The weird thing is that the steam engine has gone, there are no heavy shafts connecting our machines of work – at most, there are wires that could stretch anywhere – so why do people want us to work in the same big box together as if there was still a mighty steam engine in the basement? More to the point, why do we want to work in the same big box, for the same money, at the same speed, breathing the same air as everyone else? You won't like the answer – fear.

In the bad old days of circuses, the training of elephants was very cruel. In a way, using the twisted logic of the time, it had to be. You have a three metre high, two ton creature, with a bit of a temper; in other words, bigger and stronger and more dangerous than you. The trick was to chain the poor creature down with huge heavy chains then beat it and terrify it so that it would fight to break the chains. The chains would hurt the elephant horribly and after some time it would no longer fight against them. What the trainer could then do from that day forward would be to put the lightest of chains loosely over the elephant's foot and attach it to a weak wooden peg. It was fear that stopped the elephant from using its strength to beat its bond.

Make no mistake, you are a far more mighty, powerful and fearsome creature than your situation suggests. Really you have no bonds; you could get up right now and walk into a new free life where you could be self-employed, rich with money and rich with time. Why aren't you doing it? Fear of a chain that no longer exists. That chain used to be called job security. The truth is that the employers have betrayed us all. They claim to invest in their people, which I suppose they do, but what are they investing in, exactly? They would say 'improving your skills', but your skill to do what: to have a better life, to deal with your issues of contentment and hope? Or is it about pulling the red lever faster?

The betrayal
Back to the steam engines again. Possibly things could be speeded up and the operators could pull those old red levers faster or more accurately, so teach them or train them to do so. But because they are part of an engine-driven process, everyone has, within certain parameters, to move at the same speed. This training, then – is it investing in the people or investing in the engine that the people are part of? New cogwheels turn faster, new oil makes it run smoother, and training helps the people keep up.

This is where the betrayal comes in. The elephant trainer, however cruel, had entered into a lifelong bargain with the animal – it would be fed and sheltered for life. The red lever-puller had a job for life. In the western world, there were thousands upon thousands of mills making more or less the same products. If you didn't like the way the employer treated you, a glance at the evening newspaper would reveal pages and pages of adverts for red lever-pullers.

When I was young, our local biggest and most prestigious engineering company had its own apprentice school. You would join on a wage and be sorted by intelligence and ability – the top few would go into technical, the next group would be skilled machinists, next semi-skilled machinists, and finally unskilled (but still trained). In a way, the company made a rod for its own back because its training was so highly valued that there were thousands of companies ready to employ their engineers. Because of this, they not only offered the best training but also the best pay and conditions. That company has long since moved production to the Far East and computerized the machines. A recent technical CEO said, "In the future, all companies will have just two employees, a man and a vicious dog. The man's job will be to feed the dog, and the dog's job is to stop the man messing with the computer!"

The companies that are left are training us to be useless. Let me explain. We get training in ever narrowing areas that our employer wants us to focus on. There are appraisals that we have to suffer (yes, suffer) every few months, to see if we come up to the mark and are fully compliant on every aspect of our attitudes and skill – and even appearance. Who wrote those specifications? Our employer – or worse, some idiot consultancy firm. Who does someone who meets those specifications become useful to? Our employer. Do those specifications make us useful elsewhere or, more importantly, to ourselves? I doubt it. Our ability to precisely decorate the company Christmas tree (a genuine example, I kid you not) makes little difference to our lives in the outside world. When the work moves East, where does that leave you?

Do it yourself

Imagine, because of the fall in popularity of animal acts, the circus moves on, leaving the unfortunate elephant behind still pegged down. We would watch the poor creature starve to death, held by a thin chain and a wooden peg. Why doesn't it just walk off and tuck into the rich crop in the field next door. Why don't you?

I have been self-employed for years, with periods of having 'proper' jobs where I have worked for someone else. Those were always unhappy times that ended inevitably in a fairly spectacular fashion. This is probably because I have a screw loose but this loose screw will be at the heart of this book so I had better explain how it works.

Imagine you have a task which requires performing; painting your house or cooking your meal. You get quotes, you look at menus, sometimes you must look at the cost of the raw materials, the time involved, the expenses, and when you look at the figures you have been quoted, you say, "That is outrageous. It would be cheaper to do that myself". Can you just start to understand that is how I felt whenever I was in a job? "They get how much for what I do, sell, or make! I could do that myself and keep all the money." In other words, why are you making money for someone else?

Don't be a potato
Call me an old cynic, but I always give a wry smile when an employer says, "Our most valuable asset is our people" or, "We invest in our people". I could understand this if a potato chip company said, "Our most important asset is our potatoes. We invest in our potatoes." How do you think the potato feels? Valued? Appreciated? Safe? Do you think the potato aspires to be something greater or more fulfilling than a humble spud? I hope not, because free-thinking, self-motivated potatoes are the last thing the company requires. They may feel that a great investment is being made in them but that investment is only intended to make them better performing, consistent and reliable potatoes. Maybe a kilo of potatoes costs £1 and would, after processing into chips, be worth £10. Perhaps the other processes – the packaging and the marketing – cost £8, leaving £1 profit; therefore potato costs are equal to profit. If you could halve potato costs, it would add 50% to profits. Guess what? Chinese potatoes aren't £1 per kilo, they are 10p. Where does that leave our loyal potatoes? On the compost heap, that's where. Maybe other vegetables would command a premium

price – parsnip chips becoming the trendy snack to be seen with. Perhaps our loyal hardworking potato could retrain to be a parsnip – I don't think so . . .

The poor potato has put so much effort into being a better potato, going on potato improvement courses to achieve the key performance indicators of perfect potatodom, change is no longer an option. Are you a potato? Or even worse, are you a carrot, a vegetable that under no circumstances fits into the plan of things? No matter how many training programmes, counselling sessions or appraisals, the poor carrot can never satisfy the company. How low that carrot must feel, how useless. As with a potato chip, a carrot is doomed, but that may not be the carrot's destiny. It may be an organic carrot that has found its own way to grow, valuing every knobbly bit and unexpected outcrop, still growing and full of flavour. Not a failure, but completely and utterly in the wrong job.

UGLY DUCKLING

The story of the Ugly Duckling has always fascinated me. It seems to suggest that whilst ugly and rejected by the other ducks, one day you will wake up and become a beautiful accepted member of the group, but the truth is that didn't happen. The ugly duckling, although always wanting to be accepted as a duck, woke up and found he was something entirely different – he was a swan. He had to find happiness by leaving his duck aspirations behind and becoming a successful swan. He did find pride and happiness, but he never ever became a duck and the ducks that he left behind probably hated and feared him.

Just another brick in the wall

To drop the overstrained vegetable analogy for a bit, what I am trying to say is that modern employment just makes us cannon fodder for the machine. The global corporations may wring their hands with anguish as they lay off their people and move production to other countries, but the key word is 'global'. The people are just another raw material like iron, minerals or, yes, potatoes. Your job can be done cheaper elsewhere but then are you happy and fulfilled doing it anyway?

Speaking as a business 'guru', a very sinister trend amongst professional corporate consultants that I have noticed is the practice of process engineering. The simple concept is that, just like a conveyor making cakes or televisions which is a manufacturing process that could be improved, the human activity of an organization can also be streamlined and improved. This is your life they are messing with.

The employers would say that their training and subsequent appraisals and measurement improve competence. We should agree, of course, but competent to do what? These modern competencies are getting either more narrow or irrelevant. Corporate Christmas trees are hardly a saleable skill and are just an exercise in elephant whacking to demoralize you into submission. More of a threat to us is the specific skill that our employer requires. In this global world of mega corporations that we live in, our employer could, and often does at the drop of a hat, move production to another part of the world.

THE SPECIALIST TRAP

One of my roles as a 'jobbing business guru' is to help people get started in successful self-employment. The candidates often find themselves in my clutches quite unwillingly and unexpectedly through redundancy. The first conversation with them is about what they would like to do to earn money. We need to assess what they would be comfortable and able to do. The fancy HR word for this is a skills audit and this book should help you to do one for yourself. This is often where the trouble starts.

Referring back to the apprentice school, once we had achieved the competencies required, we had broadly saleable skills. The operative word here is 'broadly'. A skilled machinist could accurately operate a lathe or a milling machine and could make bits for everything from ships to motorbikes (few of which we still manufacture here). The computer-controlled machining centres and the export of jobs has seen an end to that, and the skills required are becoming very specific.

Let's look at a typical candidate; he has been a design engineer and has been laid off. When asked, "What now?" the first straw to be grabbed at is "consultancy". Consultancy in what? The obvious answer would be in the skill that has been so carefully developed by their previous employer. In this hypothetical case they work for a jet engine manufacturer who has moved production to China. Our chum is a specialist in jet turbine blade profile design. Is he any good at it? Yep, he is absolutely brilliant, but who on earth wants a jet turbine blade profile designer? Well, his old employer used to but they don't now because that's why they laid him off. There is no one else who makes jet turbines unless he is prepared to move to another country.

Appraisals

What a rotten trick his employer has played. Just as with the elephant, they have beaten and cajoled him into the narrowest of performances.

Let's just examine that appraisal process, cruel and unnatural treatment that it is. If you have been lucky enough not to have had to suffer one, just look at a typical one. You will be set 'by agreement' certain targets and goals. I put 'by agreement' in quotes because try disagreeing and see what happens. The achievement of these goals and targets is the subject of the appraisal. The scoring is weird in these politically correct times, as one cannot be described as rubbish or bolshie! The heart-piercing stiletto is far more subtle than that. They use words like 'met', 'partially met', 'not met' (as in objectives) or 'exceeded' if you've been good. 'Not met' is a punishment, make no mistake. Perhaps you are middle aged and middle ranking and you find yourself sitting with a fresh-faced, perky line manager from HR, who tells you piously that you have 'not met' your agreed objectives. Personally, I would rather be chained to a spike and be beaten with a ringmaster's whip than suffer the humiliation of that. So you slink away hating yourself and determined to get better, or, as your bosses would wish, more competent. Every business wants competent people as opposed to incompetent people, but the competence you are bullied into may be of no use anywhere else. Your benevolent employer is making you useless.

FREE AT LAST

There is a great book on future trends for the world by Magnus Lindkvist where he states that competence causes resistance to change. Think about that for a minute. Do you have any musical ability? Do you play the piano? If you do, then the better your natural talent, probably the more you practise. As you become more competent, you are less likely to pick up a trombone. If you are like me and have completely cloth ears, you are likely to try every musical instrument until you acknowledge you can't play any of them. Employers, whilst eager to make you competent at the task they picked out for you, also realize that you will be useless to them when they no longer need that process. So as the circus leaves town, you are left pegged out for the birds to peck at.

Lindkvist also says that we are born as individuals but die as clones. Employers need clones but you deserve to get back to being an individual. As this book helps you to become a successful individual, don't expect to become popular with the establishment. Politicians and companies have a somewhat irrational fear of the self-employed and use words like 'loose cannon' and 'unpredictable'. It is a foolish attitude really, because self-employed people can be so much more efficient, as what they sell are outcomes. The price is agreed and the job is done. Are you in a 'proper' job? When do you go home – when the job in hand is done, or at the company's stated going-home time? Do you work at your own pace or that of your colleagues? Can you get up at 3.00 a.m. if you are not sleeping and put the finishing touches to your current project so that you can enjoy breakfast in bed and a quiet read of the newspapers?

EFFICIENT

I have owned and run companies with many employees; I have been employed and now, as a lone self-employed 'guru', have determined never to employ anyone again. The pressures of my work demand help with my book keeping, so imagine I create a permanent position of book keeper. The chances of me having precisely 40 hours work of book keeping is infinitesimal so I must pay a modest annual wage and get someone a bit iffy who can stretch the work by just loping about being bored, to fit the week. In reality, what happens is that for just a few hours a week, a self-employed person, who has seven or eight other clients, does my work brilliantly and then clears off to the next job.

Keep it simple
Another huge efficiency of self-employment is the actual cost of work. I am involved with a charity that lends money to start-ups – the only loan criteria are that they must have been refused a loan by every possible lender. By virtue of this the applicants are people that society has truly written off – ex-long-term offenders, down and outs, and people with disabilities or mental health problems. Tom Peters was asked why small businesses succeed and his reply

was, "Cause they gotta". So to quote him, when asked why such people become self-employed, the answer is, "Cause they gotta." For obvious reasons, a lady who murdered her husband ten years ago and is now out of prison may have trouble finding a job.

One guy in particular had never had a job, abused a few substances, and was in effect a street beggar. He produced a child and decided it was time for a change. There was no chance of finding a job and who on earth would lend money to someone who looked and smelled the way he did. Well, we would! The skill audit was scary; there weren't any. Driving licence, none; telephone, none; home address, changeable. He wanted to do pressure-washing and would need a machine, a mobile phone, a bicycle and trailer to get the machine about, and some leaflets. The charity don't just lend the money and clear off, the applicant is mentored by volunteer gurus until they are on their feet. By the way, despite the supposedly high failure rate of small businesses, this charity rarely has any failures (the value of good advice and guidance, read on!) and gets virtually all its investment repaid. It was clear that because of this guy's lifestyle he had limitations, but by working within his scatological approach to life and without really breaking sweat, he could knock up a very steady and undemanding £100 per day over five days that took him above the national average wage. There was not much more potential for growth but he didn't want that – within the constraints of his fragile personality he was making more money than he had made in his life. More importantly, he was making enough to give him contentment and security – cheap to start and easy to maintain.

DOES HE NEED WATCHING?

Imagine for a moment that the guy in the story above was part of the cleaning team of a major corporation. Marketing would have to find the customers, Logistics would handle the bicycles, and how many of these mad-eyed individuals could one manager handle? As many as ten? Is the manager on as little as 50 grand a year? If so, that takes £100 per week off every cleaner right away. Sometimes these ordinary tasks such as window cleaning, gardening, house cleaning, sandwich making, only work as one-person bands. Whether you want one of these simple, undemanding enterprises that just keep the wolf from the door and keeps you laid back and unstressed is a discussion for later, but the point to make at this juncture is just how efficient self-employment is. What does Management's head in is the lack of control they have over us wild woolly people. If you can keep all the money you earn rather than share it with the tottering bureaucracy you work for, you will be better off.

IT ALL ADDS UP

How can this be? Do you think I am working one of those clever mathematical tricks where it appears that you have eleven fingers or you can get a gallon into a pint? How can you get more by working alone? Well, of course I am hiding something from you and that is all the bits and bobs that surround the job, that aren't actually the job itself. Again we will be paying an awful price for attaining the competence that our employer wanted, because the more focused we become, the more useless we become in other areas. If we look at our pre-industrial treadle-loom operator, he understood a number of things the current wage slave does not understand. He understood where his work came from, he knew where his raw material came from, and he understood the cost of those raw materials and how to negotiate a better price. He understood the value and price of his work and how to negotiate that to the optimum? He knew where his product was sold and about alternative places if needs be. He knew how to maintain his machines and even how to manufacture new parts for it – he probably built the thing in the first place. If you are in paid employment, how much of the above do you know and can master? Before we move away from the weaver, also understand how flexible he could be over time and money; if the price for his cloth was low, so what, that is what he got for it. If it was high, he would work day and night to fill the orders in order to stash a bit of cash for the tough times.

RIDING THE ROLLERCOASTER

Modern workers have got used to earning a regular wage that, over the years, creeps steadily upwards until the employer can no longer afford it and they get fired. In the current recession, things have been encouragingly different. People have realized that, instead of taking the random chop of redundancy as ten percent of the workforce is cut, if everyone takes a ten percent cut in wages, they can all stay. In some cases, this strategy has saved the company. However, that still has not achieved the same level as the self-employed mentality.

In my own case, when the dot com bubble was inflating nicely, there was lavish launch after lavish launch and what everyone wanted was a business guru as their keynote speaker. The fees were eye-watering and demand insatiable. One month, we had thirty jobs all over the world. My wife, who is my manager, partner, owner and harshest critic said, "What do you want from this?" I replied, "To still be alive at the end of the month." No one could keep that pace up for long and anyway the dot com bubble popped spectacularly and things returned to normal, which was about 50% of that mad pace. The self-employed can take a 50% drop in income and still be happy – or, in my case, delighted. Could you?

POINTS TO PONDER ON
'IT'S ALL ABOUT YOU'

Self-employment allows you to be paid what you are worth and it also gives you the opportunity, if correctly handled, to increase what you are worth.

- How will you manage – or can you manage yourself?

- Customers want outcomes not process. They want to know we *can* do it not *how* we do it.

- You do not need to feel tied to one machine, one place, or even one country to do your work.

- Is it only fear that stops you from being self-employed?

- Be careful if you feel that your training is an asset to you as it may only be valuable to your ex employer and may not represent all the opportunities you may have.

- If you do all the work, then you should keep all the money.

- Self-employment can set you free to enjoy being a square peg – just stay away from round holes.

- What you are qualified to do is not the same as what you want to do or, more importantly, what you need to do to make a living.

- Success will depend on broadening your skill base and flexibility.

- When you are in normal paid employment, your efforts are paying everyone else's wages as well, particularly your boss's!

- To survive, you need to budget for wild fluctuations in income.

CHAPTER 2

LEARNING AND GROWING

. . . In which we find being stuck in a rut gives us an opportunity to explore many escape routes, how even our name can become a valuable asset, learn to be agile, and don't be tempted to lease a hatstand.

STUCK IN THE MIDDLE WITH YOU

As an old hippy, one of my guiding philosophies comes from Robert Pirsig and Michael Kramer's *Zen and the Art of Motorcycle Maintenance*. I have used this example in a previous book; however, it is very relevant to our current situation. Pirsig and Kramer have this idea of 'stuckness' on the benefits of being stuck. When you become stuck you learn things. The wage slave is in a rut, but not stuck. Someone said that a rut is a grave that is open at both ends. Each day is the same, the same things are done, the same money is paid, until you are too old to do it, and then a little while later you die. When you arrive in Heaven will you regret not scoring higher in your appraisals . . . ?

Imagine you are in a familiar room that you enter and leave at will. One day you are in it and the door handle comes off in your hand. You are now stuck and this stuckness will lead you towards a number of learning and growing opportunities. You would ask yourself why you wanted to leave the room anyway, it might be nicer to stay. You would consider the mechanics of door handles. What happens when you turn a door handle? Rotary motion is converted into linear motion inside the door so that the bolt slides across. Maybe we could fashion a device that could manipulate the mechanism in the door. If there was another person outside the door we could strike up a conversation with them and ask them to use the handle on their side to let us out. What about the window? Until the door broke we had never considered climbing out of the window, but once we try it maybe it is the best and most fun way of leaving any room.

If we apply stuckness to our job we have to see how narrow our focus actually is. We tend to describe the task or function that we perform as our work. So OK, that's what we will call it for now, but later, work is going to mean a whole lot more.

Let's imagine yet another room with a desk in the middle and a serving hatch in each of the opposing walls. Through hatch number one comes our work, we take it to the desk and do our work at it. Whether that is sewing things on it, polishing it, or writing letters and numbers on it, when finished to appraisal standard we hand the work out to hatch number two. Where did your work come from, where did it go? One fateful day, nothing appears from hatch number one – now what do you do? You have no work. Or, possibly, you have done tons of work and hatch number two is locked. It won't be long before you are buried in unwanted work. What is actually going on behind these hatches; Design, Marketing, Sales, Finance, or Distribution?

In the case of the door handle, we have explored engineering solutions, we have forged new alliances and relationships, we have explored wild alternatives, mastered new skills, and become opportunists, none of which we have ever done in our job.

WHY DIDN'T IT WORK OUT?

Maybe the preceding words have seduced you into thinking about being self-employed. Hurrah! I've been self-employed most of my life and I love it but – and ain't there always a but – I meet people who fail horribly at being self-employed.

I am often hired by government departments or large companies that are downsizing to conduct courses to help prepare people for self-employment. I get to know these people and am always disappointed to find the odd one returning to some boring job after a while and telling me that 'it just didn't work out'. If you are reading this book because you are dreaming of being self-employed or about to become self-employed or you are already self-employed, I am sure you would like to know why 'it didn't work out'. If we could nail that and deal with it, surely it would stand to reason that it will work out. So let's interrogate our unfortunate chum to find out what happened.

"How do you mean, it didn't work out?"

"Well, I just couldn't find any/enough work."

There can be a number of reasons for this one; it's got a lot to do with what is behind serving hatch number one. Firstly, do you know for certain that there is a need or demand for the work that you do? Our turbine designer may have to look for something completely different to do. What do you suggest? That is going to take a lot of careful work and planning; you don't want to get it wrong again.

Do you know where to find the demand, if there is any? Possibly Mr Turbine could design blades for the Koreans – once everything is sorted out, he can work remotely using his computer in his garden shed, but first he may have to put some clean pants in a carrier bag and hop on a plane to Seoul. That takes bottle, but we now live in the world where the single self-employed person is a global business and therefore has to be prepared to behave like one.

Once we know that our work is relevant and there is a demand, can we sell ourselves and our work? These are all part of our stuckness skills. To be fair to employers, other people are working hard behind those serving hatches to get the best possible price for our work. They are packaging it in the most attractive ways, delivering it on time, and then going to war on our behalf to get the money. There are none of those things that we can't do or get someone to do for us, but those things must be done and done as well, if not better, than they were in our previous job. It is all about achieving our true value, which has to be a lot. I don't wish to get all motivational here but if you don't believe you are worth anything, you won't be able to get a lot. Well, you will get what you feel you are worth. Which is nothing.

THE PERSONAL BRAND

There is a weird paradox that I want you to solve for yourself later in the book, in the exercise of 'Fred's Garage', but for now imagine your name is Gladys Sponge and you are a watch maker employed by the world famous and prestigious Swiss 'Heuromeglex' watch company – average watch price about $5000. What in truth the customer is actually buying is a watch made by Gladys Sponge, in effect a Gladys Sponge watch – but that is not the name on the face. You decide to go freelance and make watches with Gladys Sponge on the face, a person that no one has ever heard of. As a wage you probably got $100 per watch so where does the other $4900 come from? At the end of the day, the customer is willing to pay $5000 for what in effect is a Gladys Sponge watch, as long as it says Heuromegelex on the face. So what we have to find out is how that extra value and demand is created.

The first reply that springs to mind is that Gladys' employer was a well-established famous Swiss watchmaker. That statement makes some very strong and often not very well-considered points about self-employment. I suppose that I have picked up a lot of my guruing experience and knowledge from doing it for so long and from meeting the successes and the failures, but I am sure some of my skill is actually genetic.

My Dad was a weird old Viennese psychiatrist who never really occupied the real world long enough to make any money, so it fell to my Mum, who at home was a lovely Mum, but outside was a tough, hard-nosed Cockney dealer. Her speciality was to buy run-down businesses, build them up and sell them on. She was the turnaround queen – she could transform loss-making concerns into gold mines – but even with her prodigious capacity for work she used to say that time was needed to establish a business. She reasoned that it would need at least one year's money put aside to survive, and in fact she often bought businesses that had a great idea but had just run out of cash a few months in.

A matter of time

Let's return to our failed friend, "It just didn't work out". Perhaps he just didn't give it enough time. How long did it take the watchmaker to become established? Two hundred years? Does that depress you? It shouldn't – some of the worlds most famous and established brands have not been around for as long as you might think. It is how they manage those brands that is so clever. We may even be able to borrow or rent a brand ourselves. I am sure that the mega starlet superstar isn't actually mixing up her best-selling fragrance in her bathtub with a stick and going round the shops flogging it herself. It will be some guy with a perfume factory who is renting a bit of her or his celebrity to save all the fag and bother of brand building. Gladys and her watches can become 'established' faster than you could imagine by judicious use of PR and networking. We will all need to get a bit famous.

Brand new, new brand

For us, the newly self-employed, while today may well be the first day of the rest of our lives, it's also the first day of the construction of our brand. One of the intentions of this book is to help you to choose what you would like to do, an enterprise that will keep you rich and happy to the end of your days. Well, if it blows up in the first six months it isn't going to be a lot of fun, therefore what we choose must be influenced by how long we can keep it going before it can keep us going. If you decide to buy a cruise liner for $100 million, a year's interest on the loan will probably cost a million per month or $250,000 a week, or $5000 a working hour! If, on the other hand, you have no job, no business, you will probably totter by indefinitely on the pittance you receive from Social Security or welfare. Therefore, a very modest enterprise can be sustained for a long time on modest means, and a more ambitious enterprise will require more finance. Is that an over-simplification? So why do new enterprises crash and burn in the first few months?

Time costs money

In my home town I watched with interest as a lavish refit was undertaken to construct a new coffee bar. Clearly no expense was spared to get the finest Italian barista machines and mood lighting. The job must have taken six months. There was a grand opening and a week later they were gone. How on earth could that happen? All I could find out was that the refit had taken longer and cost more than expected and the customer numbers were disappointing. DISAPPOINTING?! They gave it a week . . . maybe after a year they might have had to pull the plug, but they hadn't budgeted for a year and probably thought takings would cover loans, which they didn't.

That, then, is a key message. Only pick the enterprise or activity that you can afford. Getting established takes time, although I can show you how to hurry things along a bit with a bit of game play, jiggerypokery and sleight of hand. If you can't afford the time, you will have to modify your choice of enterprise.

BE A GUERILLA

What really frustrates me is when people have a sound idea and then destroy it by burdening it with unnecessary expense and costs. Let's for a moment get into the joyful, anarchistic and fun heart of being self-employed. You can be fast moving. You can travel light.

You can seize opportunities when they come your way. When disciplined Western troops come up against rebel guerillas, they find them surprisingly difficult to beat. When you need to move a troop of soldiers and their equipment, the logistics and support all have to move. When it is time to fight, an objective has to be presented and explained to the whole troop, who in turn have to coordinate to avoid shooting each other. If you picture the camp, there are probably vehicles, a medical centre, communications, and even a kitchen. Your opponent, on the other hand, is a raggy individual who functions completely independently with a simple reliable weapon that can be fixed by a blacksmith. He has one simple objective; to kill people dressed the way you are. He eats off the land and travels fast and light, making his own decisions. Yes, he fights in a group but they are loose-knit acquaintances who also want to kill people dressed like you. That is how they compete with what appears to be a much stronger force. That is how we can thrive by being an agile business guerrilla.

The legendary hatstand

It is at this point that we come to a crossroads. I want you to read this book and be guided to success. I would love you to see how your value as a needed resource to others can be increased.

Your perceived value to others will be governed by the impression that you make on them, which must be of the highest quality. Nothing cheap, nothing tatty, no corners cut, but apparently contradicting that is the danger of overburdening the new enterprise with too much debt and commitment. The problem is the bad habits that we learn when we have a 'proper' job. If you were in the army and had decided to become an independent freedom fighter, whilst I would encourage the purchase of a good rifle and ammunition, I might counsel against the setting up of a field kitchen.

In my book, *Go It Alone*, I tell of my experience when I encountered a group of executives who were being outplaced (sacked). Their employer, to try and assuage his guilt, set up a series of 'Outplacement' courses and seminars. The one I was presenting hoped to guide these people towards successful self-employment. A few months after the course, I visited each of them to see how they were getting on. One guy had based himself in a business centre which was magnificent with gardens, car parking, and a fantastic reception area. I was directed to his palatial office where our hero sat resplendent. He had hired a cutting edge light wood designer desk; the latest computer hummed and whined while it sent its commands to the fabulous colour printing centre that was against the wall. "How did you afford this place?"

"Rented, just one week in advance!"

"The desk? The computer The printer?"

"Leased."

Then out of the corner of my eye I saw the thing lurking in the corner, the thing that summed this madness up! It was . . . a hat stand.

"A hat stand! Where on earth did you get that?"

"I leased that, too," he replied defensively. "I always had one in my other office."

"Did you ever have a hat?"

"No."

"Have you got any customers?"

"No, but now I'm all set up, that's the next thing on the agenda."

"Are you quite mad? You have been at this for months. No customers and all you have succeeded in doing is leasing a hat stand."

It was at this point that the conversation was terminated rather acrimoniously.

THE MEANING OF WORK

Before we continue, let's investigate that word 'customer'. The people who fail at self-employment say that they failed to find work, but do they understand what work is? Work is not just effort or activity; loads of diligent people put in loads of activity and effort into their enterprise which still fails miserably. They say that they have been working hard but they still failed to find work. What on earth does that mean? Let's see if we can make it clear. Work is the effort and activity that someone will pay you to do.

In the case of self-employment, from this point on we must see that the person who will pay you for this effort is a CUSTOMER. Therefore, above all else we need to find and keep customers, people who will pay us for our effort and activity. In our previous life, someone who gave us money for effort and activity was called an employer. They, in their own way, would find and organize customers – or not – that wasn't our concern. The employer was entitled, for our 'wage', to manage and direct our activity and to punish us if we didn't produce enough of the right activity and effort. Now you are free, the customer – the person who provides the money – has no right or obligation to manage or punish, but what they can do is to see that we are possibly rubbish and walk away. No notice needs to be given, no appraisal undertaken, no warnings, just voting with their feet. Your management and directions will come from your current employer, that's you, and all activity must be undertaken with the customer in mind because that is the only place money will come from. Everything else will involve you in cost (particularly hat stands).

Agile, not wobbly

What makes the self-employed enterprise so brilliant is its agility. The crew of the *Titanic* saw the iceberg from miles away but it was already too late – such a mighty ship could not turn quickly enough, so they all just stood and waited for the crash. If an individual was in a kayak, they could paddle around the iceberg with a few seconds' notice and centimetres to spare. It's the same with large corporations; they are not stupid, they are just big. When I do my presentation of future trends in the global economy, they don't disagree with me, they are just too bulky to change direction quickly. As I do my stuff, I see their eyes widen in horror and sometimes I could swear I can see the cold white peaks of an iceberg reflected in their eyes. But don't feel that smug in your kayak; canoes are agile because they are unstable, so a few lease agreements, a nice big bank loan, and a high rent are rather like carrying a huge anvil in the kayak with you. Just one wobble and the whole thing turns upside down in a split second. To survive for those first few critical months, you must travel light.

I would be truly relieved if you told me that you could survive for at least a year without any extra income (of course we would expect you to make oodles of cash but it's nice to be safe). So our mission is to present a sharp, attractive, professional image without spending all our cash. Our goal is to increase our value.

POINTS TO PONDER ON 'LEARNING AND GROWING'

- Being stuck helps us to see the bigger picture and helps us to understand the new skills we need to master to achieve success.

- Whilst it would be great to benefit from your core skills, you must master the surrounding skills as well to achieve your full value. Don't sell yourself short.

- Build your personal brand with extreme care as it will become your most valuable asset that you may even be able to sell for cash one day.

- When planning your enterprise, make sure that you have enough financial support to last for as long as possible. If the sums don't add up, don't take the risk. Set your sights slightly lower.

- All the little luxuries and unnecessary equipment are like putting rocks in your pocket when you go swimming. Customers and income first, treats later.

- Finding and keeping customers is the only activity that generates revenue; everything else involves cost.

- Agility is related to instability. Whilst agility can be an advantage, adding a burden of debt makes the instability all the more dangerous.

CHAPTER 3

THE ROLE MODEL

. . . In which we learn how a burglar can teach us a thing or two.

THE VALUE OF GURUS

People often ask me to model the perfect self-employed person. The Buddhists say, "He teaches that which he needs to know most of all." All our image and profile stuff, our value and our ability, are worth nothing if we cannot find enough work. Enough work, paradoxically, means finding too much. This means being able to increase prices to the juiciest of levels and being able to turn away jobs you don't fancy. Even I would like to learn that one!

I am a very busy and well-paid 'guru', but there are people in my line of work who can earn $100,000 an hour and are booked for five years in advance. I wish! Therefore they are doing, or have done, something that I haven't, or they know something that I don't. If I line up ten prospective self-employed people, with no help or guidance two thrive, three or four totter by, and the rest fail (with good guidance eight out of ten succeed). Is this the fickle hand of fate? I doubt it. The failures always sing that same old song: "I couldn't find the work." We would all like to find the work, but who can?

A LIFE OF CRIME

May I suggest a life of crime (actually when I ran this idea past my publisher they freaked out, so please don't really consider being a criminal, it does have its drawbacks). The business model I wish you to consider, however, is that of a burglar. I watched a miscreant on the television who was saying things like, "Well, I was spending a couple of grand a day on me habit."

A couple of grand a day! Where on earth was he getting that from? Well, he was probably stealing it. That is the thing, while we worry about finding work, our criminal chum has no such problems. Work for him is burglary and he goes and does it whenever he wants to. That is nirvana for the self-employed, to work when you want to, whenever you want to. The burglar doesn't wait for work to come to him or to look for work, he goes and he does it, purely driven by his need for cash at the time.

A man of many talents

We have many lessons to learn from our light-fingered friend. He has a specialist area, which is burglary. He has honed his skill at house-breaking and has the tools and knowledge to execute his 'profession', but should you leave your wallet on the bar counter he will steal that too. Because he is the perfect opportunist, his core philosophical mission is dishonesty and his need is cash. He almost certainly grew up in an undisciplined and unstructured environment which has made him ultra sensitive to opportunity. He is also not hidebound by false pride and job descriptions and is prepared to take it when and where he can.

We, on the other hand, have been tied by structure and order and probably wouldn't know opportunity if it bit us on the arse.

Also, we do get a bit confused, believing that what we say we do for a living says who we are. The burglar has no such problems; in fact, he is extremely reluctant to say what he does for a living and has a life that is very separate from his 'profession'. If there is a big job to do, like robbing a bank, and if our burglar is the instigator, he will assemble a group of like-minded individuals who have the required skill sets: Molly the driver, Sid the explosives expert, Janice the alarms ace, and Brian the muscle. These kind of loose federations are extremely interesting and should be very instructive for the escaped wage slave.

The big lumps

Firstly, let's just have a look at the management structure. Management in commerce traditionally works on the septic tank principle of the big lumps floating to the top. It is rarely based on talent or ability and, worse, is not relevant to the job in hand. They say that people get promoted until they exceed their abilities. I don't want to get pompous about this book but I suppose it is starting to look at a new world order. Firstly, perhaps people could move up and down the hierarchy to suit the work in hand without fearing for their job. It is also worth considering the definition of 'ability'. It may not just mean skill or talent but also refer to inclination and energy.

There is a big hoo ha at the moment about the ageing workforce. Because governments are skint and people are living longer, the retirement age is being bumped up. At the same time, there is a whiff of legislation that will make it illegal to force someone to retire against their will. Of course, the employers are up in arms, saying that for some roles, i.e. physical ones, age is an issue, but genuine mobility could solve that.

"Tell you what, I'm getting less confident flying this thing. I think I'll take up pushing the drinks trolley up and down the aisle instead."

Can you see that happening? Well, it should, and that is why traditional employment could be doomed. It is that resistance to change which makes employer and employee alike unable to plan a happier life in the future.

Our crooked team have no such qualms and nor should we. It's Mickey's bank job, so we listen to Mickey, look at Mickey's maps, plans and timing, and give our input, but defer to Mickey and even let him have a bigger share for thinking it up. If it was our plan and our thieving opportunity that was spotted, the rest of the gang – including Mickey – would defer to us.

The workers united
A coral reef is a community of tiny organisms that together are big enough and strong enough to sink a ship. These loose alliances can be vital for successful self-employment. They cover a lot of issues, including the ability to do big things and become a global brand, and also deal with the issues of personal isolation and loneliness which can be a problem if you are leaving a busy work environment. It also gives us a skill pool of the resources we may lack personally.

If the bank job should be a success, do you think that, buoyed by their triumph, the gang would sign up to a twenty year lease on a prestige downtown office and become Crime Inc with nice glossy brochures setting out lists of the nefarious activities they would be prepared to undertake? If they have enjoyed working together, have made money, and see further opportunity, then sure they will pull another heist, but they are a long way from pension plans and setting up a board of directors.

A matter of trust
It is also worth noting that, because they are crooks, they know that they are working with . . . well . . . crooks and there is a very healthy level of mistrust. I am going to get pilloried for this but to advise you to trust no one is not a bad philosophy. No, it doesn't indicate that I am dark, bitter and twisted (although I may be), but when you go into a shop and hand over your credit card and

they ask for a pin number or signature, do you say, "What's the matter, don't you trust me?" Well, the truth is, no they don't, they don't trust anyone, but we are so used to that and the fact that it protects the security of our cash, we comply quite happily. When you start your freelance life and chums commit you to a few days of very welcome work, a little letter of commitment, some cash up front for materials, or maybe a direct debit authorization should not cause offence. If it does, it should set alarm bells ringing.

Our gang will have made very sure that no one clears off with more than their fair share, or start spending irresponsibly in a way that could bring the law down on them all. They are friends, and by dealing with the trust issues at the start of the job, they will stay friends. Also, bear in mind that our burglar can happily work alone on his own projects – the others help but are not essential.

Down but not out

Of course the best laid plans can go adrift and possibly our burglar is arrested and convicted. As a career criminal, prison is inevitable, but what happens there should be a revelation for the self-employed.

Again, let's go back to our self-employment failure. "It just didn't work out." So what do most people who fail at being self-employed do? Usually they sink into total despair, and then flap about like a headless chicken until they find a 'proper job'. Once bitten and so on, but it is rare that a failed enterprise should have such dire consequences as to land you anywhere as horrible as jail. It stands to reason that working on this principle, the mighty sword of justice will instantly encourage our burglar into changing his ways and giving up his chosen career of crime.

Here is an exercise for you:

1. Why do you think the burglar doesn't give up burgling?
2. If your enterprise fails, why will you give up immediately?

Write the answers down and think about them – contact me at www.geoffburch.com.

Again, we need to tread with great care because I am not talking about flogging a dead horse. When I did my TV series, 'All Over the Shop', where I was supposed to rescue failing businesses, I found a shop that had never ever made money. The guy had supported this loss making disaster with his savings and the equity in his house. Because he had a lot of savings and a big house he had managed to do this for fifteen years. Bonkers!

There is a very fine balance here; it is distressing when a business is abandoned because not enough time or money has been given to it but, on the other hand, there is no point in flogging a dead horse. What we have to do is to use our skill and judgement to make this very critical decision: if we bail out too early we could be missing something really wonderful but, on the other hand, there is no good going on and on throwing good money after bad. Hopefully, this book will help you to develop the judgement to make these very important decisions.

If our burglar hears the police sirens, he drops everything and legs it. He knows when to cut and run. He will abandon a project but not his vocation. He will never lose his desire or motivation to be a self-employed criminal, he is just prepared to change if he has to.

Painful lesson

Our burglar now, however, languishes in prison. He got a fairly stiff sentence, he lost his tools, and the cops have seized some of his valuables as the proceeds of crime. He sits on his hard bed, chin cupped in his hands as the morning light streams through the barred window. He then does what we should all do at moments of crisis: he starts a period of calm, uninterrupted contemplation. "What went wrong?" And, yes, "Is it time to give up crime?" Because eight out of ten career criminals don't give up crime, and about nine out of ten business failures do give up, there must be something going on here that we can learn from.

A trouble shared

Is he alone in there? No, of course not, he is shut away with hundreds of like-minded individuals, all similarly reflecting, with whom he networks and shares best practice, learning and sharing the latest techniques and identifying the juiciest targets.

"Hello, mate, wotcha get nicked for?"

"Burglary."

"How'd they catch you?"

"The cops have got this machine that can track down nicked stuff from your mobile phone radiation."

"Cor! I'll have to watch for that, I won't take me phone on the next job."

Our chum leaves prison refreshed with a list of new contacts, new techniques, and a very clear idea of what went wrong – and what steps to undertake to ensure future success. In fact, he is an all-round far better burglar. The amazing thing is that he will repeat this cycle many times but we, on the other hand, tend to stay down when we get knocked down. Please, this is not an advert for a life of crime, but it should give us some learning points.

SCHOOL FOR SCOUNDRELS

1. The dream of all self-employed people is that they will find enough work. However untalented I am, if I decided to be a rock star, as long as I filled those venues with paying fans I would keep doing it. Enough work, of course, means well paying work. The burglar chooses when to work – I wish we all had that control, but skilful marketing, selling, planning and preparation can get us some of the way there. Our goal should be to dispose of, "I wish that . . .", "It would be nice to . . ." and "If only . . .", and instead make a successful outcome inevitable. **Goal: to work when, where, and how we want to.**

2. The burglar's core skill is, of course, burgling but his 'core value' is dishonesty which he can, in times of need and opportunity, apply to stealing anything. The newly self-employed often fail to take advantage of opportunities when they present themselves. If modern employment has preceded their enterprise they cannot be blamed because there is a constant narrowing of focus. Just as the hat stand syndrome can be a symptom of clinging to the security blanket of the old ways, so purposely forcing the enterprise into a narrow focus is giving a false sense of security, a sort of commercial agoraphobia. Twee names are a classic symptom; 'Pining for the Fjords Pine Furniture' could never make an oak chair even if someone was prepared to pay for it. Broaden your horizons, look for opportunities and then grab them with both hands.

3. The burglar is more than capable of separating his life from his 'job'. When we are choosing our enterprise, definitely view the activity as a lifestyle thing that you would have fun at and would be happy doing. Choose something that meets your skill sets. Pick a course that will make you financially secure, but never ever choose an enterprise because it sounds good when you talk about it at parties. The burglar wouldn't!

4. The burglar is aware of his skills, technical or physical shortcomings, and is more than happy to recruit others, or to outsource the skills he needs.He is not handicapped by 'management issues' and a lead member is cheerfully agreed for each project simply based on skill, knowledge and merit. In self-employment, these loose cheery federations can achieve anything. You could build a ship, make a film, or drain an ocean, or rescue a small Mexican village with your gun fighting skills. But remember, just

because you worked well with someone doesn't mean it is time to form a partnership or a company.

5. The burglar works with others he knows, he sells his spoils to people he knows but, unlike us, his description of his colleagues stops at 'he knows' and never strays into our cliché of 'knows and trusts'. Bitter experience has taught him not to trust too readily. While you may be shocked at this, a large number of business failures could have been avoided if less trust had been shown. "One of my biggest customers went bust owing me thousands." "My partner ran off with the money." "They promised the order but we had nothing in writing." Just think about the above statements and consider what precautions you could have taken to avoid these disasters.

6. Getting caught, for the burglar, is a complete disaster emotionally and financially. What he does is to enter a period of quiet contemplation (admittedly enforced). He acknowledges and analyzes what went wrong and plans for the future with contingencies to avoid getting caught again. He will get caught again, of course, but not for the same mistake. When I meet the 'It just didn't work out' person, further questioning reveals, "Well, we started this travelling gourmet burger van, then we found no one would pay enough for the burgers and then we found we couldn't pitch at the big events because they are booked two years in advance." Firstly, they didn't do their homework, but OK, let's accept that now they have learnt a valuable lesson. So if I kidnapped their pets and said, "Make a success of this burger van or the tortoise gets it", they would be forced to say, "Well, we could offer coffees and hot chicken sandwiches. I wonder if the smaller events ever have hot food. We should shop around

for better suppliers." Don't flog a dead horse but alternatively don't give up too soon.

7. The burglar in and out of prison has a network of associates who he 'networks' with, sharing best practice, new technology and information. Do not work in a bubble; most people who own restaurants don't ever eat in restaurants. Brilliant! How will they ever find out what's going on?

POINTS TO PONDER ON
'THE ROLE MODEL'

- Regardless of what we have chosen as our enterprise, we should be permanently and acutely aware of all opportunities that come our way.

- Leadership and management are no longer an issue for the self-employed, but in collaboration with others we must be relaxed about who leads the project. It's about practicality, not status.

- 'Trust no one' is a pretty harsh maxim, but I have seen so many businesses destroyed by a betrayal of trust or some kind of misunderstanding, that a level of healthy scepticism is very valuable.

- We should learn by our mistakes but not get defeated by them.

- Even better, learn from the mistakes of others.

- Never stop developing your skills. Technology changes so fast that if we don't keep on learning and changing, we could be left high and dry.

CHAPTER 4

CALL THE EXPERT

. . . In which we examine the difference between consultants and experts and show how we can get real value from our knowledge. We also find how working with our hands and living in the cracks can bring joy, happiness and financial reward.

DOOMED

When, many years ago, I was coaching the outplaced executives in the pleasures of self-employment, I would go around the room to find out if anyone had a coherent plan on how they would generate revenue. I tell this story over and over again to make a different point to different audiences, but the idea is that I can smell trouble simply by going round the room and asking for people's ideas. My performance goes a little like this:

"What are you going to do?"

"Consultancy."

To myself, "Doomed"; out loud "You?"

"Consultancy."

"Doomed. You?"

"Consultancy."

"Doomed. You?"

"A tea shop in Devon."

"Let me guess, it is going to be called the Mad Hatter."

"Yes, how on earth did you guess?"

"I don't know, I just had a funny old feeling." To myself, "Doomed."

One day, after this performance a fairly agitated woman approached me and asked, "Why are consultants doomed?"

I was a bit nonplussed; no one had asked me that before. It got me thinking that probably the people in the audience who were, or wanted to be, consultants thought I was just having fun and saying that for effect, and everyone else was concerned with other things like opening tea shops. But I do think consultants are doomed.

What is a consultant? Pause here, have a think, and reply to that question. Then tell me when you will need to pay for the services of a consultant.

The truth is that, as we trundle through life, we come up against things that we can't fix for ourselves because we lack the skill or the understanding. We now have some choices; we can buy a book or a CD of instruction, or go on the internet and teach ourselves how to fix whatever is screwing life up at the moment. This is good if it is a very regular event and we have invested the time and the effort into acquiring a valuable and often used new skill. We could get someone else to show us how it is done, or we may acknowledge that we don't have the time, inclination or capacity and we hire someone else to actually do it. In the real world that is what happens to everybody. Sometimes, we just do not have the knowledge, ability or time to fix things for ourselves. When you are in such a bind have you ever felt the overwhelming desire to pay good money to consult with anyone about it or do you just want an expert who will come and fix it?

Where the consultants live

You may notice that I have used the words 'real world'. That is the world where you will be living and working from now on. The other world, the unreal one, is populated by the upper echelons of corporations and government where the motivation is self deluding, stupid or even sinister. That is where consultants live. Consultants are not individuals; in fact, we should call them consultancies. Possibly the outwardly kind and avuncular CEO of a major corporation can see that axing 10,000 jobs and moving production to the Far East could save him and shareholders 100 million or so a year. Well, this nice chap, that we even see on the TV sometimes giving sage and kindly advice, can hardly be seen to be destroying the lives of 10,000 families. So he calls in the consultant, gives them a Machiavellian whisper in their ear, a cheque for two or three million, and after a few months a 500-page report appears condemning the Western plant and showing that the company's survival depends on relocation. The CEO sheds a tear, gives a sad shrug that would shame Pontius Pilate and as he chokes back emotion tells the world that, heartbreaking though it is, one cannot contradict what is in black and white and the plant will have to close.

It may well be something like that which has resulted in you joining us as self-employed so I suppose something good came of it. For government it is a very expensive form of King's new clothesism; they need expensive smart people to tell them that the stupid things they are doing and the horrible failures they are creating are in fact the right things to do. The spectacular thing these consultancies pride themselves on is their ignorance. Just think about it: they are often offshoots of huge accountancy firms so how can they send management consultants in to show how to run a hospital? Their justification is breathtaking. Surely doctors, nurses and patients know what is needed?

"No," cry the management consultants. "These people are so close to the problem that they have become the problem. As our fine thought processes are unsullied by any knowledge of health or medicine, we can bring a fresh understanding." They can make an expensive virtue out of stupidity.

Welcome to the real world

Real world individuals and small companies are not so gullible. Therefore the consultant is dead, but long live . . . the expert! If you were considering consultancy, do not be downhearted but do be realistic. Corporations and governments have a very special hidden agenda for employing consultants, think tanks, and institutes. They want the corporate global names that charge thousands and thousands per day. No one, but no one, wants a cheap consultant, but for us mere mortals we do need to talk to an expert.

"How do I fix my computer?"

"Can you fix my computer?"

"Is this the right way to get a tax rebate?"

"Can you show me how to sell more?"

Here is a test for you: when you were thinking of becoming a consultant, do you have a knowledge or skill that would benefit and be valuable to other people so much so that they will be prepared to pay you for it? If you have some airy fairy thing about goal setting or colour me successful you may very well be on thin ice, but if you can fix my photocopier, well, come on in.

IT ISN'T WHAT YOU KNOW

Hopefully, this section of the book will help you to choose what you would like to do, happily filling your time making money for the rest of your days (well, actually, for as long as you want to or stay interested). Before you choose you have to see where there is an opportunity and whether you would enjoy exploiting it.

In Matthew Crawford's very clever book (in Europe *The Case for Working with your Hands*, in the US the book is called *Shop Class as Soulcraft*), he puts forward the case for working with your hands. He talks about the so-called knowledge economy and also the threat to jobs. To put it very simply, he says that if your job can be sent down a line, then it is most likely under threat. The doctor is safe but the radiologist isn't. The architect is under threat but the builder isn't. He goes on to say that the world we live in is obsessed with the idea of the post-industrial knowledge economy. We study and sweat and work our way through college and university to obtain ever more esoteric degrees and qualifications that result in us working in some dismal cubicle with loads of other 'knowledge workers' along with the constant threat of being fired.

JOIN THE QUEUE

This ever faster struggle to get a college education makes me think of a con that I got caught by the other day. The ghastly budget airlines used to give you a ticket and let you fight it out for a seat, the best seats going to the fit and the fast (a bit like life, then). Then some bright spark realized that they could squeeze more money out of us. Eureka! Priority boarding. For a 'modest' fee you could buy a priority boarding pass and get, well, priority boarding. I arrived at the airport and saw one check-in desk with one or two people at it and another with a queue that stretched for miles. Although I felt blackmailed I went to the ticket desk and bought a priority boarding pass. Yep, you guessed it; I ended up at the end of the big queue as they had sold priority boarding to everyone.

Perhaps we are doing the same when we go to college or university? In life, that small queue probably holds the dressmakers, the cake makers, the electricians and the plumbers. As Matthew Crawford points out, what is the knowledge economy? One must suppose this is an economy based on knowledge that people will pay for. How much will you pay a philosophy graduate whose head is packed with knowledge? As you gaze at the hairy bum cleavage of the guy who is inside your washing machine, ask yourself why he is there. It is because the machine broke and you don't know how to fix it. You would chuck a pocket calculator, kettle or radio, but not a thing like a washing machine, a car, or even a computer. The guy knows how to fix it, and you don't. When you get the bill, understand that this guy earns good money – often more than the so-called professionals, and his job can never be done down a wire. Now that is real knowledge economy!

PRIDE IN THE JOB

The other thing that Matthew Crawford goes on to claim is that to work with your hands is actually more mentally challenging than office work. As an inveterate fiddler with mechanical things such as motorbikes and, on the odd occasion, washing machines, I can accept that. One often stands and watches some delinquent machine, thinking to oneself, "Now why is it doing that?" You then have to explore the mind of its designer and run the 'What if' scenarios in your head.

My beloved pinball machine blew up one day and it was packed with a spaghetti of endless wires. I dreamed about wires for so many days and nights that I actually gave myself a temperature. I have never in my life applied so much intellectual effort to a project and when I eventually fixed it, I felt great. As wage slaves you very rarely get that sense of achievement. When I was a kid, I drove a bulldozer and built a stretch of highway. I still drive that road and can see with pride the bit I dug out.

A POTENTIAL DISASTER

I would, however, also like to reverse that thinking a bit. Educationalists claim that they are getting better at spotting potential even amongst disadvantaged kids. That is great, but let's fantasize about where that is taking us.

You know those meat thermometers that are attached to a spike? You shove the spike deep into the meat and a little dial tells you the true state of what's going on inside. Imagine you had an implement like that which you could shove in a kid's head and, regardless of class, wealth, opportunity or disability, this thing would either read 'intelligent' or 'stupid'; a device that, regardless of the kid's inclination, would give an unchallengeable measure of intelligence and therefore potential. Maybe 90% of the children tested would read 'intelligent' and surely therefore should go on to further education to gather the glittering prizes, but what of the remaining 10% quite categorically diagnosed as stupid? Should we abandon them to leave them to their fate? Of course not! The enlightened educationalists among us, while realizing there is no chance of raising their intellect, also understand that useful employment can be found for them through gentle and undemanding training. Today known as vocational training, these somewhat lesser people could learn to work with their hands in the building trade, hotel industry, beauty or mechanics. So what do we have here? Someone in the future who is clinically diagnosed as stupid, adjusting our brakes, applying chemicals to our faces or, best of all, we see the happy prospect of a stupid electrician.

Too cool for school

Worse than that, if this cursed meter has shown us to be intelligent, we get packed off to college for three or four years to learn some high-falutin', book-based knowledge from people who have never had a real job in their lives. We come out with a huge debt and a bit of paper, to do what? It is just like being in that priority boarding queue again: as you look around with your bit of paper clasped smugly in your hand, you realize with horror that everyone else has one, too.

In the old days, when college education was for the elite, one would meet some work-grimed tradesmen and realize during the conversation there was considerable intelligence there. The reaction was almost inevitable: "You are too good for this job, you should be working in an office somewhere." The trouble is, we all started to work in an office somewhere and what a dismal unfulfilling place it turned out to be.

Let's get a couple of things straight. First, working with your hands can be very effective and rewarding both emotionally and financially if those hands are attached to a brain. Second, whoopee! Skip, hop, jump and sing, you are free at last, free to choose what you would like to do to earn your living. If brainwork with paper and computer is your bag then rejoice, for together we will find you paying customers, but if, despite your bits of paper and citations, you would love to wield a hammer, a spanner or a frying pan, make no mistake that can make you rich and happy, too.

Oodles of poodles

In my book, *Go It Alone*, I mentioned a physicist who had been laid off from the nuclear industry. He came on one of my outplacement courses, and some months later I saw him, clearly prosperous and happy. What on earth does a surplus physicist do for a living? I asked him.

"So what are you doing?"

The reply was somewhat unexpected.

"Poodle parlour."

"What?" Did my ears deceive me?

"I have opened a Poodle parlour and I have never been happier. When I was 5-years-old, I could do quadratic equations. My mum told me I was destined for great things, but the problem was I hated the stupid easy quadratic equations and wanted the challenge of kicking a soccer ball. Then when I was married my wife lovingly but firmly drove me on to my professorship and doctorate by making huge sacrifices. My hobby was clipping poodles, my passion was clipping poodles, but I was trapped by the 'a man with your brain clipping poodles, never!' But now redundancy has set me free although I must confess one of my favourite tail shapes is modelled on the Strontium 90 atom."

The crazy thing is that, although his family was scared by his choice of work, they now realize that they like life with a very happy and contented man.

Consultants doomed? Without a doubt, but expertise – now that's something that we all need. Experts, however, can be very broad ranging. You may pay them to tell you if your understanding of Greek philosophy is correct, or they may come to your house armed with a big sledgehammer to bang fence posts in for you. Whichever, if you can be acknowledged as an expert, you can charge a premium.

LOOK FOR THE CRACKS

If what is put forward in this book is the truth and the only way to be saved is to be self-employed, then surely everyone will do it and we are all back in the same queue again. Well don't worry; this is a little book of secrets and golden opportunities that in percentage terms very few people will share. The perfect storm that is shattering Western commerce will probably affect about 300 million people. If one percent of those people read this book, that will make it business book bestseller of the century so already you are in a pretty elite band, and this is where the first of a series of opportunities presents itself. Crawford calls it working in the cracks.

If you are in a minority, there is always an opportunity. A thousand peoples' lives are ruined when the steel works closes, but the one person – the 0.1 percent – who stays behind to sell the scrap, becomes rich beyond his wildest dreams.

At the time of writing, we have been bombarded by the major retailers of CDs and DVDs giving profit warnings. My friend, who is a recording expert in the industry, has often chatted with me about the total demise of the retail music business with downloads, MP3 players, and online tax free sales. Yep, the end is nigh. Then I heard on the radio today that Indy record shops are booming. Well, that shot my fox, so I had a think and this is what I believe is happening. Maybe a big city centre music store needs £100,000 a week to break even, with 150 staff and a huge floor area in a prime site. Through technology they lose 50% of trade and have to close. That still leaves £50,000 per week going begging. Even if things decline further there will always be a hard core of fans who like their music bought undiluted from a place where they can mingle with like-minded individuals and where they will meet an 'expert' (that's you). My musical friend is a world's expert on getting beautiful pure sound on to cassette tapes, and is mourning their passing with good Eastern European gloom, but even he admits there must be millions of cassette players in the world. If he is the last person creating great products for them, he might just find a gold mine.

POINTS TO PONDER ON
'CALL THE EXPERT'

- However you describe what you do, do you know what the benefit is for your customers?

- Don't be a consultant, be an expert.

- What is it that you know that your customer doesn't, and can you be paid good money for it – even if it is how to fix their washing machine?

- Doing things and making things that you can see the results of give you an enormous sense of pride.

- Just because you are intelligent doesn't mean that you can't find joy and fulfillment through working with your hands.

- Great qualifications give you a choice – make sure you choose to be happy.

- If the feast was big enough, the table scraps can leave a banquet for us.

CHAPTER 5

THE PROFESSIONAL GAME

. . . In which we bust the myths on what work is, where and how we should do business, and look at the conflict between professionalism and price.

WHAT SHALL WE DO NOW?

This is all leading us to the great enterprise opportunities and the choices we need to make. Before we go into too much detail, perhaps we should take a moment to clear the decks and square some things away.

To become successful we must explore opportunities, be aware of threats, and exploit the world as it is. A great business guru (in truth, actually, a number of great business gurus have said the same thing) said that there are only really three ways an enterprise can succeed. The first is remarkable excellence, second is a niche, and third is to be unchallengeably the cheapest. A sort of third and a half, in my mind, is to be innovative, to have something new or a new way to do something that others haven't offered.

(Warning, someone also said that pioneers are people you find face down in the dust with arrows in their back). Being the cheapest is also a bit of a dodgy option as well, but stay with me, all will be revealed.

At the same time, I have been inspired by three books which, on the face of it, have conflicting messages. I have already mentioned Matthew Crawford who says you can find happiness by working with your hands, but then we come to Timothy Ferris whose book, *The Four Hour Work Week*, comes up with the very tempting prospect of joining the New Rich or N.R. as he calls them. Finally, we have the future trend expert, Magnus Lindkvist, with his book, *Everything We Know is Wrong*.

Join the new rich

Timothy Ferris gives the impression that he is one of the sparky West Coast computer whizz kids. His new rich differ from the old rich in this way: old rich people just had money; new rich people need three things to qualify – money, time and mobility. To explain, if you earn £100,000 a year doing 80 hours a week, someone who earns £100,000 a year doing four hours work a week is richer. Someone who can do it in four hours sitting on a beach in Bora Bora with a laptop is richer still. The book goes on to show how by creating virtual business and outsourcing the boring drag of actually working you can make a good easy living.

Of course, it's all a bit more complicated than that, but here is a story to illustrate his. I was on a trip to Mexico where I encountered a fairly dumpy and unprepossessing couple of tourists who frequented the same internet café as me. I won't spoil their enterprise by giving the exact details of their business, but let's call it Gnome from Home.com where they sold garden gnomes online. The lumpy woman (for she was the mastermind) would go to her site and squeal, "Look Kev, another 20,000 orders!" She would then forward them to the Chinese factory that would dispatch them. That was their business and New Rich they were.

I have a theory which states that to really make a fortune you do need to be a bit stupid. If I paid you to bounce a ball, say, a dollar a bounce, how long would you keep it up for? Some people could do it forever. Me? About ten minutes, before I got bored and desperately wanted to do something else.

THINK LIKE A SHARK

The expression 'a bit of a shark' suggests how cunning the subtle, deadly hunter of the deep is. The truth is that a shark has a brain the size of a walnut. If you challenged it to political discourse or the design of electronic circuits you would defeat it every time, but fall in the sea off Bondi Beach and see how you get on in a swimming and eating contest. Swimming and eating is what a shark does, it doesn't get bored or distracted because it doesn't have the equipment. The problem is that you do – you're bright, sparky and enthusiastic. Perhaps that's why you are considering the freedom of self-employment. Therefore, when choosing your enterprise you must consider whether you will get mind-numbingly bored, and if you can live with mind-numbing boredom. If you have worked in a large corporation you have probably lived with it up until now without the financial compensation self-employment can bring. The only trouble is that now you are free you won't have the iron carrot of corporate discipline to stop you wandering.

Simple
So when I suggest that for some of the simpler business models you need the mind of a shark, what I mean is that once, after the fine tuning, you find an enterprise that works, you don't screw it up by tinkering with it.

I met a very rich guy once and thought he was a bit simple (fact is, he probably was). Again not to reveal his exact enterprise, we will call him the balloon man. "What I do is sell balloons from a kiosk in shopping centres."

"Wow!" I said. "You could sell ice cream and toys – and you could locate in cinemas as well."

His empty eyes turned to me, his soft mouth hung loose (with maybe a touch of drool).

"What I do is sell balloons from a kiosk in shopping centres."

Realizing a dead end, I asked, "So how many shopping centres are you in?"

"One thousand, eight hundred."

What is it they say, "If it ain't broke don't fix it." My trouble is I would want to fix it even if it meant I had to break it first.

A LIFE IN CHAINS

A very harsh thinking mega retailer said something very tough to me once and that was, "Small retailers are small because they are crap. If they weren't crap, they would be chain stores."

He was wrong, of course, but he did have a point. If you have a simple clean formula for making money you can repeat it over and over again. Some small enterprises don't expand because they don't want to, but an awful lot don't expand because they are barely hanging on by their fingertips just doing what they are doing.

Stop here for a moment and decide why you are doing what you are doing. Maybe like the burglar you just need to feed your habit? Only in your case the habit is maybe a mortgage and kids. Or you want to do the whole lifestyle, "They hate us 'cause we're free, man" stuff? If you just need the money, let this book help you to assemble an activity that, after its setting-up period, will just make predictable amounts of cash. Just don't be tempted to mess with it when it reaches optimum performance just because you are bored. Also bear in mind the burglar probably does enjoy the excitement of burgling. So no fun at all is probably unlikely.

Hopefully, though, together we can go beyond that and actually change our life for the better as well.

WHEN GURUS COLLIDE

The collision of the three books I mentioned have literally given me some eureka moments. Timothy Ferris has suggested in the *Four Hour Work Week* that, literally, as long as you can connect your laptop you can be anywhere in the world making money, like my Gnome from Home.com friends. Matthew Crawford suggests that working with your hands is preferable because if your job can be done down a wire it can be threatened by anyone in the world. Magnus Lindkvist in *Everything We Know is Wrong* suggests that even the tiniest enterprise can be a global player, so I suppose by combining the conflicting books you could hand-make traditional corn dollies and sell them from your laptop all over the world.

The online barber

A bit more realistically, when I saw Lindkvist giving a presentation he mentioned his barber. He said his barber was OK, not the dearest, not the cheapest, not the best. His punch line was something along the lines of "If I could get my hair cut over the internet, this guy would be toast.". This comment brought a great reaction from the audience (and from me). The point is that, however small our enterprise is, we are now also global players and our competition is global. That is very possibly why your current job is under threat if you process insurance claims that could be done in India for a dollar an hour, or if you weld shipping containers that could be done in China for a fraction of what you get paid.

Handyman

But hold on there for a second, let's just run that again. If you could get your hair cut over the internet that guy would be finished. But

Self-Made Me

here's the thing, you can't get your hair cut over the internet. That guy will never be toast for that very reason. Perhaps as we choose our enterprise, unless we want to take on the world, we should pick something that can't be done over the internet.

This reminds me of an awful old joke. A guy describes himself as a handyman.

"Can you paint?"

"Not very well."

"Are you any good at gardening?"

"Not really."

"Cooking?"

"Nope."

"Well, what's handy about you?"

"I live just round the corner! Now that's handy."

A shark in a puddle

The hairdresser wasn't the cheapest or the best but may have been the nearest. Where danger lies in this situation is if the barber next door is better. The message is that we must be far better than our competitor, however big or small our catchment area is. Clearly, if what we do can't be sent down a wire, we live in a small pond in which to be big, but a shark in a puddle will soon get hungry. The bigger the hunting ground, the more potential there is, but the more competition there will be. Whatever you choose, you must be streets ahead of the competition.

THE NATURE OF WORK

So now you are going to choose what to do, what sort of enterprise will suit you? Apart from crime which we have already dealt with, to my mind there are two sorts of enterprise: you can be a taxi driver or a coffee table maker. If you have never had any desire to drive a taxi or possess no aptitude for coffee table making, please allow me to explain.

60

I use each one to represent the way we could earn our living. In the case of the taxi driver, once he has bought his car, his enterprise costs him relatively little until someone pays him to work. In other words, the taxi driver does no work until paid. As a business guru, I fall into that category, and so would a hairdresser, physiothera- pist, business expert (remember, not a consultant), accountant, or lawyer – and possibly mechanics and plumbers.

The taxi driver's problem is finding what we describe as work, the activity that someone else pays us to do.

Work smart not hard

The coffee table maker, on the other hand, could go to his or her garage and make coffee tables from dawn until dusk. I am sure you can already see where this is going. OK, so now you have a garage full of coffee tables. If you make anything on spec, from biscuits to toys, you will always face the same problem which in turn creates a problem for us in the definition of work. If our coffee table maker staggers back from her garage at midnight covered in sawdust and we ask, "What on earth have you been doing?", the answer would be, "Working!" Well, previously we have defined work as an activity that someone else is prepared to pay us for. Therefore, could I suggest to the coffee table maker that she hasn't been working but merely expending effort – possibly wasted effort – unless something is done about it. In other words, until those coffee tables are sold and she has received the cash, her effort has been in vain. To quote an old sales trainer: "Nothing happens until somebody sells something".

The speculation cake

Before we deal with these issues, it should be understood that we could have a foot in both camps. If you make wedding cakes, it would be a bit daft to construct a two metre high, seven tier, white and pink confection, with 'Happy Days Kev and Doris' iced on the top, if you didn't actually know anyone called Kev and Doris, who had in turn commissioned said confection and in doing so had paid a hefty deposit. But the problem still remains for the coffee table makers that when at a loss, they tend to indulge in futile activity and call it work. But don't worry, there will be a solution.

Pretty rank

To get back to the taxi drivers, I had a fascinating conversation with my team over this and we came up with some surprising ideas which sort of support what I have been thinking about new self-employment. Let's see what your thoughts are.

Imagine a railway station with a taxi rank outside. Before we even get started on the taxis themselves, this idea of a taxi rank raises issues. In most provincial towns, the local taxi drivers give the impression of pathological laziness, where local taxi driving is a semi-viable alternative to getting a proper job. On sunny days they can be seen lolling across the roofs of their cars chewing the fat with the other taxi drivers, or even sitting in deck chairs reading the newspaper. They are self-employed, so what's going on, what has gone wrong with the cut and thrust of commerce?

The best place to hide a tree is in a forest. The best place to find a tree is in a forest.

The first thing for us, the potential customers, to consider is where are we going to find a taxi? Why a taxi rank, of course. While this may seem obvious, it is counterintuitive to the aspiring entrepreneur. Whenever I work with people who want to launch an enterprise they always feel it is important to be well away from the competition. Great idea, but it can result in you being a long way from the customer. I had one guy who felt that he had invented the wheel when he showed me his plan for opening a Belgian chocolate shop. He glowed with pride as he expressed the uniqueness of his plan. "There is nothing new about that," I said. "There are thousands of Belgian chocolate shops."

"Ah ha!" he said with a manic glint in his eye. "I have a cunning plan," whereupon he showed me a map of the country which was covered in a rash of red pins. Each one apparently represented a luxury chocolate shop and, dribbling with excitement, he pointed to a large bald patch devoid of pins. "Here, look," he capered, "not a luxury chocolate shop for miles in any direction." What he was pointing at was an area of the country that was one of the most deprived, wrecked and depressing post-industrial areas in the whole nation. While you may brand this guy an idiot doomed to failure, we fall into the same trap in a milder and, I would suggest, therefore more pernicious form.

THE KNOBBLY STICK

If you are reading this book to get inspiration for your future prosperity, I would like you to complete the following exercise. Find a fairly hefty, preferably knobbly, stick and when discussing your plans with loved ones, life partners or friends, every time you utter the words, "What this place needs is a . . ." hit yourself smartly on the head with the knobbly stick, working on the theory of Pavlov's dog – and hopefully you will eventually stop doing it. Together we are going to find out 'what this place needs' by careful research and measurement and not by listening to our hearts or our idiot friends.

The best place to find a curry

The reason taxis gather in a taxi rank is because that is where the paying public have been conditioned to expect to find a taxi. When people ask me where would be best to open a restaurant, I may well answer, in a street full of restaurants. In London, if you want a good hot curry, the Bangladeshi community are the people to provide it and you find many of their restaurants in Brick Lane.

Imagine, then, that you and I go to the famous Brick Lane for a curry. How do we choose which one to go to? Because of Brick Lane's reputation, it is clearly the place to find a curry (also it is clearly the place to open a curry restaurant, think taxi rank). Hopefully, we have had a recommendation, but if not, what about appearance, are the locals eating there, is it busy, does the menu look right (plenty of choice but not too much)?

Think about this situation because this is going to be you soon, standing shoulder to shoulder with the others. Why should I pick you? When you see deserted enterprises they certainly weren't picked – can you see why? As you try and work this out, don't for a moment consider price. Brick Lane is a strange and exotic place with quite unexpected and challenging dishes. YOU DO NOT WANT TO EAT IN THE CHEAPEST ONE.

Fair competition

What makes the taxi idea fail as an enterprise is that there is no competition. If a rank (in every sense of the word) driver decides he wants to work harder and more competitively, he can't. The drivers come around on a strict queuing basis and have a fare fixed by the local authority. There nearly always seems to be an over-supply of cabs. In a normal commercial environment this would provoke competitive activity where drivers would have to offer better value to attract customers, and yes, although I hate to say it, some price cutting at certain times of the day.

IT COSTS A LOT OF MONEY TO BE THIS CHEAP

Why I am so price sensitive is that cutting prices is the easiest and laziest way of getting into trouble. Being the cheapest is a valid company route, a strategy that some very powerful, ruthless companies with a lot of clout have adopted. It may be an option for us but I doubt it, and it requires constant attention and consummate skill. A prime example is Ryanair, who, when you book on the website, doesn't have a 'buy' button, but a 'buy my cheap ticket' button. Charging to use the bathroom on an aircraft, charging for printing boarding passes, have made them fiercely unpopular and controversial. We, as a team, have made it a policy never to fly with them because we can't stand the hassle, but the other day I was on a Swiss Air flight and as I received my free bar of Swiss chocolate I said, "I'm glad I'm not on Ryanair!" Wow, that's good branding; they might not be popular but they must be Europe's most talked about airline. They are the cheapest or certainly are believed to be, but they are also tough and powerful and are armed and ready for anyone who would be stupid enough to undercut them. Could you do that, because that is the only way that cheap can work?

A TRUE PROFESSIONAL

While we all like to save money, let me tell a cautionary tale. Imagine you go to your doctor who informs you sadly that you need major surgery. Because you are worried, the public health service is not an option so you determine to find a surgeon. Where would you look? It's taxi rank time again. The famous Harley Street in London is where medical experts gather. You wander up the bit where the thoracic surgeons collect and outside an imposing edifice sits a classic white Rolls Royce (nothing flash, just desirable). You walk into the rooms of Sir Edward Sharp-Blade, where you are met by a stunning beauty in a crisp nurse's uniform who offers you a fresh frothing latte, as you wait just a few moments before being ushered into the presence of the great man himself. (One of my favourite advertising slogans for a private health insurance company was, "Doctor, the patient will see you now!") He exudes confidence, competence and class, views your notes and X-rays, and after examining you himself, sits back and smiles so reassuringly at you.

"Yes, well, this is an operation that I pride myself that I am particularly adept at, and one that I have done many times before.

There is absolutely no need to worry, it is a relatively short operation and then you would have a few days at my clinic where I can just keep an eye on things and you will be as right as rain. In fact in my experience, patients feel better than they have felt for a long time."

You put the big question, "But how much?"

"Oh," he replies, "it is not expensive, the operation, the anaesthetist, and say, three days in the clinic, the whole thing should come to little more than £50,000."

"How much!" You leave, chastened, to think things over. As you discuss this crisis with your chums in a bar, a little man wearing glasses like Coke bottles sidles over.

"Oh hello," he says in a weird, high-pitched voice, "I'm sorry to butt into what is clearly a private conversation, but I thought I should introduce myself. My name is Cyril Spoggins and I am chairman of the Reading Amateur Surgery Club. I am a tax inspector by trade but I do a bit of bowel resectioning in my spare time. We meet above the Nag's Head bar on a Tuesday evening – would love to have a poke around inside you, there is no charge and you'll get a piece of quiche Lorraine afterwards, if you survive!"

Not at any price
Well, will you go ahead? No? Why on earth not? You are going to be saving yourself 50 grand. Oh, how that party piece of mine makes people chuckle, but up until now I have never really disassembled it to find out why you wouldn't choose to take Cyril up on his generous offer of help. What are we doing to prevent your potential customers choosing NOT to choose you?

Why don't they choose you?
First take the idea you have in mind; are other people currently making good money doing what you are planning to do? (Remember pioneering is a risk business.) If the answer is yes, why aren't those people choosing to give their money to you and if we find the answer, is there anything we can do about it? Clearly the eminent

surgeon has experience and is established (pause for thought, why do we believe that?).

Just have a think about this for a moment. When you last went to the doctor, he may have said, "Just slip your clothes off and lie on the couch." Who else in the world could just tell you to get naked and be met with total obedience and no comment?

"Because he is a doctor," you reply.

Is he? Think of your current doctor, what evidence do you have that this person is a doctor? Have you ever dared to ask for proof? What made you decide that Cyril was not competent to conduct a perfectly safe and satisfactory operation?

The first thing that has happened is that we have gone back to our Brick Lane curry house thing. We look for our consultant in a street of consultants to the point that these eminent people take pride in naming themselves after the street. You can't get better status than 'Harley Street Surgeon' or, I suppose, 'Savile Row Tailor' or 'Madison Avenue Advertising Agency'. Therefore, the first point to realize is that if we are somewhere appropriate for our activity it can boost our credibility and put us where the customers are.

Judged by appearance

Next is the personal appearance and confidence of the surgeon, to the point that we are so reassured that we have no desire to ask for his credentials or previous experience. Remember we mentioned that he was established – the truth is that we don't actually know that, but his professional demeanor just made us assume that.

This is exactly how conmen function – I am sure you are aware that 'con' is a shortening of 'confidence'. The trick is to get the victim's confidence. What is more instructive and useful to us is not how Harley Street wins, but how Cyril failed. We have wonderful uplifting, beneficial and delicious things to offer, so let's not have any conscience or worries about getting every bit of confidence we can from our potential customers. Cyril approached us in a bar to offer delicate surgery. He admitted that surgery wasn't his 'day job', his dedicated lifetime's work. The word that got me twitching was 'amateur'. Then he cheerfully acknowledged failure with the 'if you survive' crack. This is a wild and ludicrous exaggeration but it is there to make a point. Is there anything about what you offer that is not completely professional?

Professional – this is a much overused and misunderstood word, so here is a micro-dictionary:

Professional – someone who does it for money.
Amateur – someone who does it for no money.

Just for fun

So if I describe someone's enterprise as being a bit amateurish, I might not be criticizing but just stating the fact that they are doing it for no money. I think it might be fair to suggest that amateurs in the accepted sense of the word do it for fun. A definition set I want to avoid is:

Professional – someone who does it for money.
Amateur – someone who does it just for fun.
Self-employed – someone who does it for no fun or money.

AND SOON THE LAUGHTER STOPPED

Here is a little warning. If you do something for fun as an amateur, if you turn it into an enterprise it will very soon stop being fun. If you make model airplanes or embroider hilarious tee shirts, in the future you will be doing that as work. Work is the activity that someone else pays you to do and that person is called the customer. If you hate painting bi-planes red, tough, because if that is what the customer is paying for, that is what they will get. If that little bit of appliqué took a little longer than expected, then expect the customer to tell you off – that is the nature of the game. Some of the old hands at the self-employment game purposely do not damage the pleasure of their hobbies and keep them very separate from their enterprises.

POINTS TO PONDER ON 'THE PROFESSIONAL GAME'

- The new idea of riches isn't calculated in money alone but in cash, travel and time. You should aim to be rich in all these.

- Even if your enterprise is a great money spinner, if it is so boring that it makes you want to abandon it or mess with it, be very careful.

- To see if your formula is successful, you can test it by seeing if it is repeatable, even if you don't want to repeat it.

- If your business can be done over the internet, the world is your customer – but the world can also be your competitor.

- Before you start working hard, understand that the only work we are interested in is the work we get paid for.

- Don't be afraid to locate your enterprise in an area of similar enterprises. Just make sure yours is the best.

- Being the cheapest is not a guaranteed way to make a customer choose you.

- Your degree of professionalism sets your price in the customer's mind, and a lack of it creates fear.

- Don't be shy to call yourself a professional, maybe it will remind you that you are doing it for money.

- It can be fun to turn your hobby into a business but be prepared for it to stop being fun when it turns into a job.

CHAPTER 6

SHOW ME THE MONEY

. . . In which we examine how our customers search for value while avoiding risk and how we manage their expectations whilst avoiding the guidance of idiots.

GOOD VALUE

I have done a lot of work into why people buy things and what they buy, and while this book is in no way a business or sales grimoire, it may not be a bad idea to understand what might provoke people into giving us money. What people buy is value. They will not part with their hard-earned cash until they perceive value.

You may decide to become a business expert and offer to improve the sales performance of your potential client. The offer may be that on a turnover of £500,000 you could guarantee a twenty percent increase after training the sales team. That would be an increase year on year of £100,000 and your fee for the programme would be a mere £20,000. Surely then, on the face of it that represents excellent value? But here's the rub: most of my sad "it just didn't work out" and "I couldn't find any work" people had very similar propositions and failed to make anything of them.

Let us return once again to Cyril Spoggins: what held you back from signing up for the services of the Reading Amateur Surgery Club? Let me define here exactly what value is. The secret cabal of global business gurus put forward this formula:

$$Value = benefits - cost.$$

Possibly the value-containing product may be a new car so let's replace value in the formula with a Ford:

$$Ford\ car = benefits - cost$$

Maybe the benefits are all the things you would expect from a Ford car:

$$Ford\ car = all\ the\ usual\ standard\ bits\ and\ bobs\ and\ accessories - cost$$

The cost may be £20,000 but a garage may offer it to you for £19,000 so now we have:

$$Ford\ car = bits\ and\ bobs - £19,000$$

This, if everything else is the same, is a better deal. The customer loses nothing and saves £1000.

$$Ford\ car = some\ bits\ and\ bobs\ and\ free\ servicing - £19,000$$

Same car, same price, but an extra benefit.

$$Ford\ car = some\ bits\ and\ bobs\ and\ someone\ you\ like\ and\ trust\ who\ is\ nearby\ to\ look\ after\ it - £19,000$$

Now the benefits are becoming emotional and are getting tricky.

Before we look at that we could also have:

$$Mercedes = bits\ and\ bobs - £19,000$$

Same price, same benefits, but a higher perceived value car – therefore a better deal.

They just don't want to risk it

There may be a car the customer's heart likes better. The problem for us a little way down the line may be that we have identified our potential customers; we have identified a need (surely everyone can see the logic of improved sales); we have approached them and quite frankly they have firmly decided that they don't want to do business with us. They don't want to give us their money and they want nothing further to do with us. Well, for you to succeed WE HAVE GOT TO PUT A STOP TO THAT. The old cliché is that our customers are voting with their feet and they are voting not to do business with us. Let us then throw another formula into the pot for us to consider. What customers actually want is: MAXIMUM BENEFIT WITH MINIMUM RISKS

In other words no matter how much Cyril Spoggins piles on the benefits of his surgery, the perceived risk is too great. What risk is it that your potential customers can see that is keeping them from doing business with you? More to the point for us is what perceived risk, real or imaginary, is it that your potential customers can see? Maybe you make wedding cakes. I am sure you believe that the key is to make deliciously unforgettable and beautiful wedding cakes. The problem is that until the customer's wedding day has come and gone they do not discover the truth of your brilliant excellence. All they can see is risk, the risk that you will clear off with their money; the risk that you will fail to have the cake ready for the big day; the risk that the cake will look awful; the risk that the cake will taste awful and give everyone food poisoning.

LET THEM SEE THE EVIDENCE

Reflect for a while, forget your current plans, and imagine you are starting the wittily named 'Ends in Tiers' cake company – remember 'starting'. What will the happy couple think when they find you or you approach them? Address all of those perceived risks and deal with them.

Here is a little bit of help: it is no good making promises or giving verbal assurances because they won't believe you. Even money-back guarantees can be a bit dodgy – a bit of cash back for a cake disaster does not save a ruined special day. You have to convince with evidence and it must be the evidence of the customer's own eyes. In just the same way no one wants a cheap surgeon, no one wants a cheap special day. That doesn't mean that as a one-person band we can't offer fantastic value. Great value is not the same as cheap.

Marketing is going to be something we are going to have to deal with, but for now I would like to disassemble a couple of marketing clichés. One is 'exceeding the customer's expectations', and the other is 'under promise and over deliver'. Actually they are both pretty stupid or, in truth, pretty sinister because they are phrases that are not meant for the big lumps in management or even the customer, but are a bit of whip cracking for the poor old wage slaves. If you are a disengaged, bored bit of cannon fodder on the minimum wage, the big lumps believe that nailing posters about the place with phrases like, 'The customer is King', 'Passionate about underwear solutions', 'Going that extra mile', will somehow make the dismal soul-destroying job have meaning and you will work harder, with no extra reward. Actually, thinking about it, the middle ranking, office-based person is even more susceptible to this crap, with the added misery of appraisals.

Well now, the world has changed, because for us, when 'The customer is King', 'We are passionate and we go the extra mile', a big fat reward drops into our pockets, not our bosses'.

What amazes me is when one-person enterprises succeed in being slipshod, rude, unreliable, grubby and unprofessional (talk about shooting yourself in the foot)!

Fairly low expectations

So what have I got against exceeding the customer's expectation? Well, it's not going to be difficult for the Reading Amateur Surgery Club, or 'Ends in Tiers' to do that because the customer actually expects sod all. We win customers by creating great expectations, assurances and promises of great things to come. I am sure that people who survive Cyril's scalpel are delighted to have saved thousands of pounds and the happy couple who gaze in awe at the towering pink and white confection are thrilled. Of course they are thrilled and of course their expectations are exceeded.

I often get irate small enterprises, that I have been a little critical of, flap bits of paper in my face showing me testimonials from happy customers. I usually fuel the fire further by suggesting that they are happy and relieved customers. Worse than that, these particular customers must be nutters as who else but a nutter would risk Cyril or 'Ends in Tiers'. This jaundiced theory is often borne out when I meet these much vaunted 'customers', stark staring bonkers every one of them You do not want these people as customers. You want the middle and top end customers, the people who buy Ford and GM to Porsche and Aston Martin.

In Communist East Germany they made cars from compressed cardboard that were propelled in a cacophony of noises and noxious smoke by a two-stroke engine. There are people who still delight in driving those things, they declare themselves delighted. They probably drink their own wee and sing folk songs. YOU DO NOT WANT THEM AS CUSTOMERS.

We have to create expectations that are high and then deliver those spot on with precisely what is expected. (Just maybe a little unexpected bonus of a tiny bit of over delivery but don't go mad). Maybe the next cliché should be 'over promise and over deliver'.

Remember, for the new enterprise, the potential customer's default position is to expect trouble. If just looking at you reinforces that belief then we are going to struggle to succeed.

IT DOES WHAT IT SAYS ON THE TIN

Please indulge me by coming back to the previously-mentioned taxi rank for a moment where we all wait for business. Imagine that this is now unregulated and we can put forward any offer to attract the customers. I put this exercise together using the examples below and showed it to my colleagues. After a bit of discussion we ended up with a weird conclusion. But anyway, read on and see what you think.

There is the taxi rank; leading it up is a Rolls Royce with a liveried chauffeur and on the back seat is a small wicker hamper of goodies and a miniature bottle of good champagne. The delicately embossed cards suggest that a ride to town will cost around £50. I would suggest this guy would get regular work from high tipping wealthy customers.

Next, there is a clean and modern family saloon driven by a clean and tidy person. The price for a trip into town is £10.

There is also a very ancient, very rusty, big old car, with one missing window that has plastic taped over it, multicoloured and patched paintwork, and the door tied with string. The driver looks like a biker, and painted on the side with a big brush and whitewash it says, 'Into town for £1'.

I set these descriptions up with the intention of showing that no matter how cheap you are, if you are unprofessional and scary, people won't do business with you.

A surprising reply
However, this scenario was put to my colleagues and I asked for comments. Everyone agreed the attraction of the Rolls Royce. Then I said, "Who on earth would get into the scruffy car?"

The replies came thick and fast: "Students would", "I might give it a go in daylight!"

I had a think and decided that if I was in jeans and maybe not alone, I might 'give it a go'. The situation would be further exaggerated by the quantities of taxis – one Rolls Royce, one old clunker, and maybe twenty clean saloon cars. In other words, the smart saloon cars form the herd and the Rolls Royce and the clunker capture the niche at either end of the market.

I invented Cyril Spoggins a few years ago and since then the world has changed in every way, in wealth, in tax, in status, and it is the middle that are taking the bashing. Maybe the clunker does not conflict with my concept of professionalism. The fare is just 2% of the Rolls Royce, but you can see why – what you see is what you get. They can cram six or seven students into a car that cost nothing, that's £7 per trip. If the smart saloon was £1 then you would be suspicious. The old banger is precisely right for its market. It delivers what is expected – a very rough, uncomfortable but cheap ride into town.

Only the best will do

This new world order seems to suggest that firstly to be the 'est' is very beneficial. The b-est, the cheap-est, the clear-est. In these ghastly TV talent shows where they show the crowd of 'one million hopefuls', something that must be borne in mind is most people can actually sing quite well. So, when they get the fifty or so to show on TV, they only show the brilliant ones or the truly awful ones. They never ever show the quite good ones. Be the best or the worst but don't ever be 'quite good'. There are too many scrambling for the crumbs.

For every hundred philosophy graduates, there is one person who knows how to unblock a drain. I have needed that person so much more often than I have lusted after an explanation of Descartes. That also suggests that niches are a good place to be. If you can seize a niche for yourself you stand a so much better chance.

AN EXCELLENT IDEA

There has been a lot of talk about excellence, and in fact Tom Peters wrote the business book for the 20th century, called *In Pursuit of Excellence*. Every company back then jumped on the bandwagon of excellence. They started using the word in their strap lines, mission statements, and even on their headed notepaper. One idiot even rang me up and said they wanted me to set up a programme of uncompromising dedication to excellence for his company . . . and then added that this would obviously have to be done within the confines of a very tight budget. Cheap excellence, then?

That's Remarkable

For the 21st century I have seen a very much better idea. I can't remember which great business thinker came up with this one, so apologies in advance for not giving credit. The thing they came up with was not being excellent but being remarkable. That means that people remark about us. If you are a one-legged tap dancer then you are probably remarkable. If you are a beige taxi in a rank of twenty other beige taxis, you are not remarkable.

Stop right here and have a think about what you offer that is remarkable. What is it about your offer that will get people talking about you? Beige is the new black, or in other words, the colour of doom. The middle ground is the dangerous ground. It may feel safe to be one of the 20,000 people in vest and shorts at the start of the marathon but I only notice the Ethiopian who is one hour ahead of everyone else, the wheelchair athletes, and the huge purple chicken – the rest are just scenery and not remarkable.

LOOKING FOR WORK

The advantage of being a taxi-type business is that your potential customers can reject you before you get to do any meaningful, or in any event costly, activity. The key question that we must ask the taxi-type business before we move on is why haven't you got any work? Mrs Johanna Trembly, tomato blight consultant (sorry, expert), sits by her phone. The leaflets are distributed, the presentation made, and nothing has happened. No work for months. Firstly, if you read this book carefully you should not have got into this situation but, OK, so supposing you have. What options are there? What happened? What went wrong? It always amazes me that people can sit and watch themselves slowly die.

Why tomatoes?

Let's take this situation apart very carefully and see what's happening. What provoked Johanna into tomato consultancy? Is it because all she knows is tomatoes, or is it because careful research has told her there is a clear-cut demand for tomato consultants? I think it might be the former, in which case if there is no demand Johanna may have to consider doing something different. Doomed activity is still doomed even if the level of that activity is increased.

Because of my built-in dismalness I can smell trouble. In a premises where restaurants always fail, I saw yet another new one: 'Family run Eastern European Cuisine'. "Doomed," I thought. And guess what? I wasn't wrong. It crashed and burned in less than six months. What research, what public opinion, what professional assessment of demand was undertaken? Or was it knobbly stick time: "What this town needs is a restaurant serving Eastern European cuisine!"?

THE WINNING TICKET

Is that how successful businesses are started? Yes! Did I just say "Yes"? I did, but now let's examine this statement; did all lottery winners buy a lottery ticket? Well of course they did. If you want to win the grand jackpot should you buy a ticket? Yep. Will you win? No. When companies like Wal-Mart or Tesco open a new store, they are not buying a lottery ticket, but by following the elements of their careful plans they win every time. Your future prosperity is not something to gamble with. The problem is that the media idolizes the commercial successes of the people who have climbed from poverty to billionairedom – but these are lottery winners. When you ask them how they did it, they can't tell you. Sure they can pile on the platitudes and clichés – "I believe in myself", "I wouldn't be beaten", "I kept my nose to the grindstone and shoulder to the wheel" – but if you ask whether they could write a one to ten point instruction sheet on the practical aspects, they can't do it. They try: "Um, point one, believe in yourself, point two, shoulder to the wheel." "No, I want to improve the success of tomato growers. Who should I contact, where should I start, should I have an office, is there enough money to be made just from tomatoes?"

"Well, as long as you believe in yourself . . ."

It is about as much use as asking a lottery winner how to win the lottery. The cards fell right for them and that's it.

PIGEON ENGLISH

An interesting scientific experiment was conducted on the way people try to connect activity to outcome. The first thing that was required was a creature that is as stupid as a human being – the nearest scientists could find was a pigeon, a creature which is nearly as daft as we are. The pigeons were given food at completely random intervals and just occasionally, by sheer coincidence, they may have been standing on one leg or nibbling its bottom. This coincidence caused the birds to develop a sort of irrational superstitious connection between the act and the food, and the scientists noticed that pigeons would increase the amount of one-legged standing or bottom nibbling in the hope of increasing the supply of food. Bizarrely, if there was no food coming at all the pigeons would continue to leg-stand or bottom nibble in the futile hope that it would produce a reward. The potential self-employed person should be very careful not to imitate the actions of somebody who has become successful through sheer luck but somehow believes that their bottom nibbling or one-legged standing is somehow linked to their good fortune. It's worth noting that when these people go bust they continue bottom nibbling in the vain hope that good fortune will return to them but they are very rarely able to replicate their initial success which was purely a fluke in the first place.

THE IDIOT'S GUIDE TO THE TOP

People close to me (and not so close to me) accuse me of making outrageous statements with no evidence, one of which is that idiots become CEOs by default. I am often challenged on this assertion, and to support it I have come up with what I call the sperm theory of management, a route to the top that is about as much use to us as talking to 'successful entrepreneurs'.

Imagine that you are team leader in a big organization and one day HR phone to tell you they have a fast track management programme. Can you send a candidate from your team, your hard, finely honed team of brilliant individuals who work as one? You look from earnest face to earnest face, their craggy jaws illuminated by the glare of their computer screens. Can you spare any of them? Then, in a corner, you spy the desk with a rubber spider hanging over it, the hilarious bullshit alarm button, and the sign that says, 'You don't have to be mad to work here but if you are it helps'. You pause and then, "I've got just the person for you!"

"And that," I say smugly "is how idiots get to the top."

An endless supply of idiots

This is not enough for my audience; psychometric testing, fatal accidents, appraisals, disastrous mistakes – the idiots can't survive, but don't you see, they don't all have to. In any large organization there are millions of idiots and only one needs to survive. If you speak to the sperm which fertilized the egg it will say things like, "All that matters is being first", "Second is the first loser", "Believe in yourself", "Keep your nose to the grindstone and shoulder to the wheel" (do sperms have shoulders?). In an organization there is a huge ejaculation of idiots and just one makes it.

The problem for us is that we have a complete reversal of that situation; there is just one of us and millions of things that could go wrong. We don't need to know what went right; we have to predict accurately what might go wrong. Don't speak to your aspirational hero about your future plans but instead speak to the guy with the hairy dog, the one that buttonholes you at street corners and says, "Spare any change, please?" If you ask "How did you get here", unlike the successful person they will have a very clear idea. "It was the drinking what done for me", "I went into partnership with someone who ran off with my money", "We used to make radio valves and laughed at the idea of microchips". Go to the bankruptcy courts and trace an enterprise's dive to destruction. Was it avoidable? Should they have started in the first place? If you were in their place, would you have ended up in the same situation? Hindsight? Hindsight is possible when you use other peoples' troubles.

NEVER MAKE THE SAME MISTAKE TWICE

Our burglar is a very dangerous individual because, however stupid, he doesn't make the same mistake twice. Sure he will end up in jail over and over again, but he won't go down for fingerprints again or for trying to sell a nicked TV to a cop, or trusting his ex wife to keep quiet, plus in jail they share tales of woe so the mistake avoidance is multiplied severalfold. If your enterprise goes painfully bust, your next one might go, too, but not for the same reasons. Even better, it's a good idea to talk to dozens of people who have failed for dozens of reasons and learn from all of them.

POINTS TO PONDER ON
'SHOW ME THE MONEY'

- Just because you are cheap, it doesn't mean you are offering good value.

- Can you in a reflective moment see what risks your customers are taking by doing business with you – real or imagined?

- The poor old customer doesn't expect very much and is still disappointed despite that.

- Just because your current customers are happy, it doesn't mean normal customers will be, and they are the ones you need to expand your enterprise.

- Whether you are prestige or budget, your offer should be tailored precisely for your customers. Make sure you can see customers before you start tailoring.

- What is it that you do that gets people talking about you?

- If you want to be rich, don't ask a lottery winner how to do it.

- If you want to know how to avoid trouble, speak to people who have been in trouble, not the ones who have escaped.

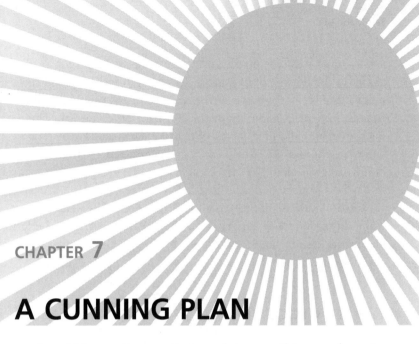

CHAPTER 7

A CUNNING PLAN

. . . In which we discover that work is something we have to get paid for and how we can achieve real value for ourselves, our enterprise, and reap the benefits of a bit of positive pessimism.

SOMETHING IN THE WOODSHED

Now we can turn our attention to the coffee table builder. This is the enterprise that can make or do things without apparently needing customers. The taxi doesn't move or work until it has a customer. The coffee table builder has decided that what the world needs is more coffee tables (or brilliant water saving devices, or sausage rolls, or home grown cabbages, or books on business!). I think shops may also be coffee table makers by proxy in as much as you will end up with stuff that costs you time and effort, and needs someone else to pay you for it before you make a living.

Let's just examine our shy little elf who has decided to become 'Coffee Tables are Us'. Whilst employed as a bank clerk, sanity (or a fair copy of it) was preserved by the woodworking shop in the garage at the bottom of the garden. Tea trays, towel rails, and cunningly fashioned fruit bowls were presented to apparently delighted friends, but the passion lay in the construction of intricate, marquetry decorated coffee tables. When the dark shadow of redundancy fell across our friend, he was encouraged by friends and family to 'go it alone'.

"Why not make and sell those lovely coffee tables?"

Why not indeed? But here is a better question. Why? The money from the redundancy has enabled the purchase of some better woodworking machines that would have seemed an extravagant and distant dream before.

THE BUSY FOOL

There are two reasons for reading this book; firstly, as a bit of gentle entertainment on a long flight, and secondly, perhaps with a genuine hope that the content will help you to become successfully self-employed. If it is the latter, perhaps it is time for you to do a bit of thinking.

Very carefully imagine that you are the proud principal of 'Coffee Tables are Us'. Firstly, what is the job? What work will you be doing? The big pitfall here is to imagine that it has actually got anything to do with making coffee tables. The first few weeks will be ones of pure, unalloyed joy, the greatest pleasure is in the making of coffee tables and you have to stock up, don't you. Golly, the work has been hard and tiring but as you clamber into bed at night, too tired to brush the sawdust from your hair or even notice the throb of blisters on your hands, somehow deep inside, although exhausted, you are purely and thoroughly happy. The contented happiness of a happy idiot.

Remember, remember, remember, work is an activity that someone else pays us to do. Who is paying you to make coffee tables? Why did you think anyone would pay you to make coffee tables?

PRODUCTION MINUS SALES EQUALS SCRAP

Many years ago, amongst the weird enterprises I had acquired, I owned a couple of scrap yards. These places, apart from breaking redundant machines and vehicles, were far too often the graveyards of people's dreams and ambitions. We have hauled away literally tons of ornamental cheese boards, clever kitchen gadgets and abandoned shop stock. Sometimes, the owners themselves would deliver their shattered treasures to sell for pennies and cents, things that had cost them their life savings or even their homes. At other times, the stuff came through the Courts, the Sheriff or the Bailiffs, but whatever, it was a heartbreak for someone. How on earth did they get into that position and, more to the point, how can you emphatically avoid it?

OH, WHAT FUN!

A big initial danger is the sheer brilliant fun of first setting up our enterprise; maybe a shop would be fun, hey, why hire a builder – we could paint the place out ourselves. If our whole working life has been spent in formal business attire, a pair of dungarees and a paintbrush will feel so new, so liberating. Let's crack open a bottle of rich red wine and on the rug by an open fire think up that clever twee name. What fun, what larks, what a slippery slope to disaster.

It's hat stand time again. While we fart about with paint brushes, stupid names and spending money, we don't have to face the fact that no money is coming in. I know, opening a shop is great fun; you have an empty shop and your savings. This makes everyone love you. The shop fitter wants your money, the landlord wants your money, the till salesperson wants your money, and last of all, the people who sell you the stock want your money. They will treat you like royalty – you are a customer – and spending money is fun. However, this thunderous outgoing tide has to stop and reverse pretty smartish or you will be high and dry.

THEN WHAT?

The coffee table builder will be locked in that garage every night doing 'work' until they cannot move for coffee tables or until they are buried under coffee tables. Then what? Remember, this is your exercise. Then what?

Planning is something that should be done. It is something that I will show you how to do, to predict trouble before it happens, to see what is the correct enterprise to start and where to start it, and to avoid risk as much as possible – none of which has been done in our coffee table exercise. So let's take it from where it is now, which is, to put it simply, 'up the creek'.

Why this is a valuable exercise for us is that it goes to the core message of this book, and that is our value as a person. The object of this book is to increase our value to a point of easy prosperity for you, the reader. The wage slaves' oft-heard cry is that of being undervalued. As I have already stated, in purely financial terms it is unlikely that a shrewd or successful employer is likely to pay you more than you are worth but then, what are you worth? Again, in very basic terms, it is very easy to value the coffee table maker. That person is worth precisely what the public will pay for the coffee table. Forget raw materials (which we shouldn't do because if you get that wrong you will be in trouble), but if it takes 10 hours to make one table we can divide those hours into the price to get a simple idea of our value. Our hero can try for £400, giving a comfortable £40 per hour. This price may never be achieved but pride tells him to stick to his guns until concerned neighbours find his starved and desiccated corpse surrounded by hundreds of unsold coffee tables.

He could, on the other hand, reduce the price until the tables sell at, say, £50 each, giving a fairly dismal £5 per hour. Although this may seem disappointing, I have seen products that, in the end, could not even be given away.

A DIFFERENT WAY

So let's take another look – we have opportunities. First question, are the tables selling easily at £50? Does that mean you can sell all you can make at £50 each? Please note right here that we should not be in this situation. We should have discovered before we started making the stupid things that the market price for coffee tables is £50. If we knew that, we may not have started but now we have, what can be done? If you could make them twice as fast that would double the income . . . even better, with unlimited demand for £50 tables, send the designs to the Far East and have millions of them made for £5 each.

If people aren't prepared to pay more than £50 for our table, we have to ask why not. Are they prepared to pay more to someone else? Is it where we sell them that's the problem? Is it how we sell them? Perhaps the customers would pay more for a different design? What is fascinating about this exercise is that the only reason we are doing it is because our coffee table maker is in trouble. As we solve these perceived problems, the person's value, in other words, our ability to generate income, will increase.

What is strange is that so-called successful enterprises don't do this. Instead of improving value, they rest on their laurels – and be warned, laurels are a very toxic place to put tender parts of your anatomy. Why the coffee table exercise is provoking so much thought is that it is an exaggeration. This exaggerated position is one of total stuckness that is provoking thought and exploration. It is when the examples are not exaggerated that we could find ourselves in danger.

A SIMPLE ASSUMPTION

There is a truly ghastly saying that comes from the age of the old 'foot in the door' salesmen and that is, "Don't ASSUME because it makes an ASS of U and ME", but let's just apply it to my favourite bête noir, twee names.

Imagine you decide to become an undertaker. Wouldn't it be fun to call it 'Stiff as a Board'? No, of course it wouldn't, we can laugh at that crazy, offensive example. Let's imagine, then, a true professional, someone who has thought things through. Maybe a personal trainer whose careful and well considered programmes can help people get fit and lose weight in the privacy of their own home. Nicely attired in a well cut and badged tracksuit, this person arrives in a clean, modern sports hatchback car with subtle gold lettering saying 'Call Home Trainer for fitness and gentle weight loss in your own home'. That's much better, what a contrast to 'Stiff as a Board', so much more restrained and well presented. Really? Why do you think that? Possibly the neighbours would peer through their net curtains, see that car outside your home and say, "Just look at that, it's about time old fatty got some help." Does that start to convince you that both are wrong? But hang on, maybe 'Stiff as a Board' will appeal to the daring and ironic amongst us; perhaps undertakers are just too dismal with all the black and purple and hushed voices. Let's put balloons outside as well and wear tee-shirts that read, 'If you gotta go, you gotta go!' Sound good? The point is that all of the above I just made up. As I explained the benefits and the pitfalls of each of those ideas you may have agreed with me, but the dangerous thing is that I pulled those ideas out of thin air – and that is not a good foundation on which to start an enterprise. Whatever you are planning must be based on hard facts that you have obtained through diligent research; good ideas are a swamp that can suck you down without trace. A huge number of enterprises are started on stuff that's made up, loads of "What this place needs" and "I've got a great idea". These are assumptions based on very little and yet people bet their homes, their savings and their futures on it.

THE MADNESS OF BUSINESS PLANS

As the wrecking crew of tattooed heavies from my scrap yard demolished yet another dream, I wish that I had summoned up the hard-hearted courage to ask the tearful owner, "What made you think that was going to work?"

There is a little piece of madness that is supposed to help here called 'The Business Plan', although personally I think it makes things worse. It leans towards the perception that if it is in writing it must be the truth. The idea is that before you start your self-employed enterprise you write a business plan based on projected figures that are supported by desk research, whatever that is. This futile exercise is usually provoked by a bank or a small enterprise adviser. You may think I am being harsh but what I want for you is success. I don't want you to lose your shirt and be sad in a few years time because your business plan misled you.

My first experience of these things was, yet again, many years ago. We needed a huge machine that could literally shred cars into fragments (strangely enough, called a fragmentizer). The cost of these things runs into the hundreds of thousands of pounds, so we toddled off to the bank for a bit of cash. Before they would hand it over they insisted on a business plan, so I sat and burned the midnight oil gauging the financial benefits of crushing 100 cars per hour. The Bank looked at my prediction of £30,000 per month in increased turnover and said that it didn't justify the loan. I asked what would justify the loan and they replied that it would need at least £40,000 so I scribbled over the £30,000 and wrote £50,000. "You can't do that," they cried, "where did you get that figure from?"

"Same place as I got the £30,000 from, out of my head. That's what everyone does with business plans; they make them up to suit the situation."

"Well, I suppose you're right," they grudgingly admitted, "but you're not supposed to let us see you doing it, that's just not playing the game."

PLAN TO FAIL

Ricardo Semlar, a hero of mine, made a very telling point about business plans which actually proves that they are useless. He said, "How come you never find a pessimistic business plan." I can't remember his exact words but the theory is something like this. All enterprises write a business plan that is supposed to be an accurate model of how the business will perform. As half of all enterprises fail or underperform, half the business plans, if accurate, should read, "Launch enterprise with £50,000. First year turnover £60,000 less set-up costs, rent and interest payments – break even. Second year turnover £70,000, profit £5000. Third year, double raw material costs, drop in sales, rise in loan rates, turnover £45,000, loss £20,000. Fourth year, call in the Receivers." As this happens to millions of companies, how come we never see that in a business plan, ever? How many times have I heard the conversation, "I have asked around and there is a demand for at least 100 of these things a week. I can make ten per hour so I could make a week's supply in ten hours."

OK. Let's imagine at the very worst we get just 10% of that, we could still break even if we sold eight. Oh, I see: "At the very worst"! Let me tell you, you cannot imagine the very worst What ever worst you are thinking of, even worse is waiting for you.

How big is your bucket?
When I was a kid, there was an advertisement in the local paper looking for blackcurrant pickers. The pay was £1 per bucket. That was a huge amount of money. A fabulous new bike was about £20, just twenty measly buckets and it would be a new bike for me. I bet I would have to hurry to the job because surely the world could

see it was literally picking money from the trees. Surprisingly, when I arrived at the windswept and muddy field there didn't seem to be too many people, but mostly craggy weatherbeaten locals who strangely didn't seem to possess the accoutrements of being the millionaires they surely were. These were the questions I had failed to ask. First, how big is a bucket? Go on, have a think, write my business plan based on your concept of a bucket. Well, these things were the size of an oil drum.

An interesting scientific fact here is that things get bigger faster than you think with more awful consequences. A two metre hot air balloon doesn't work because it only has a lift capacity of eight cubic metres. You may think that a four metre balloon is twice as big but it contains 64 cubic metres. The relevance of this to me is that the same thing was happening to the blackcurrant bucket. In other words, a bucket twice as big was 64 times harder to fill.

The second thing that I missed is that commercial currant bushes, unlike the nice big garden ones, are about half a metre high. So there I am, dragging a huge barrel through the mud on my hands and knees, and after a backbreaking day of wet misery I had a quarter of a bucket which had mostly blackcurrants, some mud, and a lot of leaves in it. The farmer refused to pay me anything, explaining that although the currents were destined for the jam factory they didn't require them to become jam in the bucket.

Don't get down, there are ways of ensuring success without risk, but we can't depend on good ideas and hunches, we are going to have to collect hard evidence.

There could be trouble ahead

You may feel that the preceding part was a bit downbeat, and I am sometimes described as pessimistic. To me, however, there are two kinds of pessimism; the sort that so frightens you with all the dreamed-up monsters that you never set out on your journey, and my sort where the idea of monsters is actually quite exciting, the journey is going to be a cracking adventure and a real adrenalin rush, but where a good solid monster-whacking stick is something to keep gently swinging at your side, just in case! The 'Titanic' was a great adventure to build and sail, and to be on the fastest and most powerful liner in history to try and beat all Atlantic records was a brave and exciting thing to do, but to fail to put enough lifeboats on it because you thought it wouldn't sink was just plain stupid. The people you leave behind in your old job are too scared to set foot on another transatlantic liner. You are brave, heroic and intrepid – just count the lifeboats.

I love and enjoy going to a play more than anyone; I get the same pleasure as the rest of the audience, it's just that I sit near the fire exit. When we plan our enterprise we should try to avoid any predictable (or, if possible, unpredictable) situations that we haven't got the tools and resources to get out of. Remember again the burglars and their ability as opportunists; if we get trapped in situations that we can't change, it limits our opportunist flexibility. Even the most successful and lucrative enterprises have not turned out quite the way the founders anticipated. If you tie yourself to a 25-year lease on a fish and chip shop, you may find that your biggest seller is pickled eggs, so maybe you should have started the Acme Pickled Egg Company. Then you find you either have to surrender your opportunity, or try and get into the ghastly business of using the law to unwind the lease, or sell on the business.

The learning points here are detailed below

First, by being modestly careful and, yes, just a little bit pessimistic, you can survive those first months or even years until your enterprise presents its unpredicted opportunities and morphs into a gold mine.

Second, try not to do things you can't undo, particularly at the start: hire and borrow rather than buy. Negotiate tough rent-free, lease-free periods. When you start your enterprise it can be so much fun giving your money away – people who want that money will be so nice to you. It will be the nicest part of the whole adventure. Think about reversing that, get tough, scrounge, beg, borrow and share, make the front bit hard work and even a bit embarrassing about the amount of brass neck you need to get what you need.

Then enjoy freewheeling to the finish with pocketfuls of cash. If, when you are setting up, someone keeps smiling at you, they will probably shortly be trousering your cash. Remember, when you are starting out, receiving smiles cost you money.

Third, become a real nuisance with your enterprise, be embarrassing with your constant talk of it and become a real enterprise here. I know it goes against what you believe and your kind shy nature but that's where opportunities come from. One day as you recount your pickled egg story for the four hundredth time, someone will say, "Do you know, that's strange, my Uncle Frank is pickled egg buyer for Wal-Mart. They have just lost their supplier, give him a ring." And you have realized pickled egg heaven in just four hundred slightly embarrassing steps. We hate those people who blow their own trumpet, those people who insist on giving out business cards at strictly social events, who drive away in their Aston Martins. Maybe, just maybe, a thick skin is something worth cultivating.

POINTS TO PONDER ON
'A CUNNING PLAN'

- Be careful if you are tempted to turn your hobby into an enterprise.

- Who is going to pay you for the 'work' you are doing?

- The most enjoyable part of an enterprise can be spending the money. The toughest part is getting the money. We are doing this to get money, not spend it.

- Your customers will only pay you what they feel you are worth, not what you feel you're worth.

- Even if your self-employed enterprise is successful from the off, you should always examine it and find areas for improvement. It doesn't have to be wrong before you start to put it right.

- Don't assume anything. Do your research.

- Don't believe that you have anticipated the very worst that can happen. There is always something 'worse' than that.

- Expecting trouble doesn't make you a pessimist, it just makes you a realist. It doesn't stop you enjoying yourself, it just keeps you safe while you are doing it.

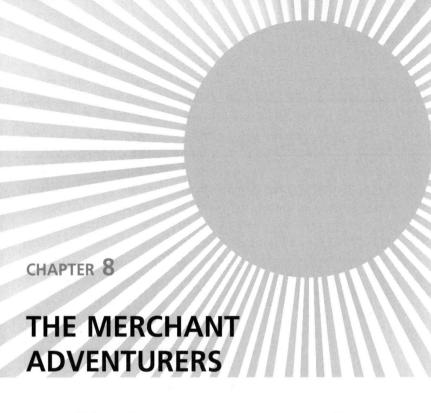

CHAPTER 8

THE MERCHANT ADVENTURERS

. . . In which we discover we can make money by selling other peoples' stuff but we also realize we don't have to buy it.

A NEW SPECIES

As much of the book so far has been about avoiding risk, it is probably worth bringing into the equation a new sub-species that can either be coffee table or taxi depending on the level of risk they are prepared to expose themselves to. These are the merchants, which include shops, mobile sales and caterers, or maybe restaurants, agents and bureaus. Strangely enough, in most of life's rich pageant increased risk can bring increased reward, but in the case of merchants this doesn't really happen, and risk can be a bit daft and should be avoided. For instance, you may wish to open a shop selling coffee tables, let's call it 'Cappuccino on Legs'. There was a really great horror film from the 1950s where the baddy could conjure up a horrid flesh-rending demon with a curse written on a bit of paper. Whoever was carrying the paper would meet the demon at the appointed time, a sort of infernal pass the parcel. Now shop stock can be a bit like this. Remember, our friend who makes the coffee tables thinks that work is going to the shed and making more and more coffee tables. A bit like the Magic Porridge Pot, that person is stuck with the fatal curse of tons of unsold coffee tables. You, the proprietor of 'Cappuccino on Legs', take the curse from them by buying the coffee tables. Or do you?

TAKE IT EASY

You may well be considering becoming a merchant, as many people do. I want you to become my friend, I want you to like me and see me as helpful so please forgive me and don't feel that I am being harsh when I say that being a merchant can be the lazy, and therefore dangerous, option. What is the perfect business? Making things can be tough and expensive, mending stuff demands expertise and special tools, being an expert can mean not getting paid and too much travel. Hey, I know what, it would be great to let someone else make stuff, we could put it in a room, and people would come to us and give us cash to take the stuff away.

More of this later, because of course it is not that easy as the thousands of boarded-up shops testify, but for now, do you really need to own the coffee tables? The coffee table maker is desperate; by buying the stupid things you could ruin two peoples' lives. Yours, because you end up with tons of coffee tables you can't sell, the coffee table maker's because you have convinced the poor sap that the things do sell so he makes even more, leaving you both with coffee tables you can't sell. Why not go to

LET SOMEONE ELSE TAKE THE RISK

The anthem of the successful trader should be entitled 'Sale or Return'. This is even more important if the goods are perishable; if you aren't bothered you could wait fifty years to sell a table, but a ham sandwich or a cutting-edge laptop is a very different story.

this desperate person and scrounge a free coffee table to put in your show area, then see if you can take orders for them. By doing this, you are letting your supplier take the risk of holding the stock.

For some time, I wrote a column in *The Grocer* magazine about various successful and not so successful convenience stores. The size of these places or the affluence of the surrounding area didn't seem to affect income as much as the shrewdness of the owner. The smallest and most successful one I visited was in a tiny triangular store, no bigger than the average bathroom. There was no room for stock and little room for customers either The only real advantage for this micro-shop was that it was on the approach to a busy railway station, a great place for papers, sweets, snacks and, best of all, sandwiches, but there was nowhere to store or prepare them. There were a few delicious-looking sandwiches in a nice variety of the best flavours – and strangely, the owner of this store never ever seemed to run out, however big the demand. The turnover of sandwiches ran into hundreds and hundreds a day and yet there never seemed to be more than one or two of each flavour. The secret was that when they ran low, they whipped 50 yards up the road to the not so well placed sandwich shop and bought more at a considerable pre-negotiated discount. They bought so many that they even had the cheek to arrange with the less well located store to have their own custom labels put on them. The point is, that by only buying as many as they sold and by avoiding waste they were able to outsource the risk of holding stock – a dream for any merchant.

FAIR SHARES

You could outsource risk but there is a price to pay and someone has to pay it. They say that when the shit hits the fan it doesn't get evenly distributed and this is the same with the profit and loss of being a merchant. If you make something that is stocked by a merchant we have to consider a few things, such as whether the merchant's key skills are marketing and selling in a way that you are unable or unwilling to do. If we make coffee tables in, say, Scotland, a merchant may be able to corner the whole Mongolian coffee table market for us. Without the merchant, it would be very unlikely that Mongolia would be open to us. We would have the problems of distance and culture to combat, therefore best to let the merchant take on Ulan Bator. What we must understand is that the merchant shares our money. If it costs us in time, effort and raw materials £50 to make a table that has a sale price of £100, that £50 profit has to be shared (that's why 'direct to the public' type ads are supposed to attract us with thoughts of bargains). This bit of simple arithmetic is not as facile as it seems because if you are a coffee table merchant you have two tough negotiating jobs to do: one is to push the price from your supplier down, and the other is to push the customer's price up. The power of charisma to increase margins is something most merchants lack in spades.

So if you are thinking, like many, of becoming a merchant, you must become truly adept and brilliant at selling. Better than you are now, better than you have ever been, better than your customers, better than your suppliers. Your brilliance at selling yourself and your enterprise will bring you great riches, but if you are not up for that please, please have a rethink.

MY SIDE OF THE STORY

What I manufacture is knowledge. I have knowledge and secrets to share and that's how I make my living! I give out my secrets, knowledge and ideas to audiences, who hopefully are entertained and profit from these ideas. I use a merchant to sell that product for me all the time and they are called Speaking Agents. They are in touch with far more potential clients all over the world than I could ever be. They are better at selling me than I could ever be because they are detached and can be objective for their customer. They also take a very modest percentage of the final fee. If you want to hire me it is unlikely that you could come direct to me to save money because it would upset these valuable agents – and they could also offer my competitor to these customers. So for me as a maker of ideas, my merchant is a double-edged sword, but one I can't live without.

THE EMPIRE STRIKES BACK

Now let's make things really confusing, because you can be a coffee table maker and a merchant. Let's say that, against all odds, the demand for coffee tables is huge. As a self-employed person you have reached a very important crossroads. The whole point of this book is to show the individual how they can enjoy prosperity by employing themselves. What I have been referring to throughout this book is 'the enterprise' because I have been studiously and intentionally trying to avoid the word 'business'. Businesses are monsters (sometimes benign) that, by virtue of their design, grow. They grow and grow until they employ you and you've got a proper job again. Therefore, when the coffee table boom occurs, you have to make a choice between two options – one of which will waft you away from my tender care in this book. You could start employing people to help you make the coffee tables; this is the start of a business. With that you must assume responsibility for those peoples' place of work, their mortgages, their welfare, and when the coffee table crisis hits, you must take responsibility for those people and their problems as well as your own.

The alternative or second choice is to become a merchant on top of being a coffee table maker.

Master and commander

Let me explain this as carefully as I can because this is the key to success in the whole self-employed thing. Taxi driver, coffee table maker or, yes, even burglar, if we can truly master the art of merchanting we can almost guarantee success. What bothers me is that so few people do actually MASTER the art. At the heart of this whole book is the concept of achieving our true value or, better still, more than our true value – and by that I mean our value in cash terms, to be paid as much as we are worth or even more than we are worth. We may feel that it is outrageous that professional soccer players are paid £200,000 per week. "No one is worth that," we cry, but if someone is prepared to pay them that, then that IS what they are worth. They have found a customer (someone who pays them) who will pay that much for their work (the activity that they get paid for). What the true and skilful merchant can do is to find work for themselves and others. They can achieve the best possible payment for their and others' work.

I have a friend who really is a taxi driver; I pay him to drive us about to our jobs but, more than that, he is very skilful at finding taxi work where others can't. Therefore he finds more work than his own taxi can handle. This means that he is able to be a taxi merchant and any work he can't handle he farms out to other taxis. Of course, he keeps the best jobs, and if work is short he is the last one to stop getting it.

It is a strange thought but if you are a merchant you will be providing others with work and you will be achieving their value for them. If you have a shop full of other peoples' coffee tables and you are achieving a good price and you have created a high demand for them, the people who made those coffee tables will be achieving their value through your efforts.

EVERY BURGLAR NEEDS A FENCE

Even our friend the burglar needs a fence, a person who can launder their money or sell their stolen goods. If you consider the character Fagin in *Oliver Twist* as a merchant, he motivated the activities of his whole gang.

So now you have some tough decisions to make. Whatever enterprise you may be considering you will have to assess your potential as a merchant. If you feel that this is not for you then you must find someone who can merchant your work. You may have had one in the past; it is just that we tend to call them employers! There is nothing wrong in the idea of having someone who can merchant your work; in fact, at the very start of this book we identified that the key problem of being self-employed is finding enough work. The problem, as you may have already discovered if you are here through redundancy, is that the merchant can also withdraw the work. They make their money from the difference between what they can get paid and what they can get away with paying you. If they can get the work done cheaper elsewhere you could be in trouble, like when the big employer merchant moves their work to the Far East.

Then, on top of all that, there is always the problem that they might not be any good at being a merchant either. So if you need to use a merchant make sure that you stay vigilant about what they are achieving for you that you currently feel you can't achieve for yourself.

GET OUT AND DO IT

What scares me are the people who set up as merchants in the shape of shops, coffee shops, garages or agents, and who have no skill or inclination as merchants whatsoever. A merchant is someone who, through the force of their skill or personality, makes things happen, who can conjure demand for work by their own driving mental effort. Although I have used this many times I think it all can be summed up with a tee-shirt I had when I was a hippy. On the tee-shirt are two vultures. One vulture is saying to the other vulture, "Patience, my arse! I'm going to go out and kill something!"

The other day I walked past a sandwich bar that had been open for a few months and, despite being what should have been the busy lunch period, the place was deserted. The people inside were standing around like very sad and very lonely vultures indeed, waiting quietly and patiently for the customers that would never come and the doom that surely would. I felt like getting in amongst them and shouting "Get out there and make it happen." How, you may ask? The skill of merchanting ourselves is one we need to aquire – this skill will help us to choose our enterprise, to place it geographically, to price it, to market it, and to drive it upwards.

POINTS TO PONDER ON
'THE MERCHANT ADVENTURERS'

- Being a merchant should not be seen as an easy option.

- If you fill your store with stock you paid for, you are taking a big risk. Sale or return passes the risk to the supplier.

- Merchanting is a skill, one that has to be learned and mastered for real success. If you think it's about sitting waiting for the money to roll in, you are in for trouble.

- If you've got a great idea or product you may consider using a merchant rather than becoming one, particularly if selling isn't your thing.

- If the work or business isn't coming to you, either give up right now or go out and get it – those are the only two choices you have.

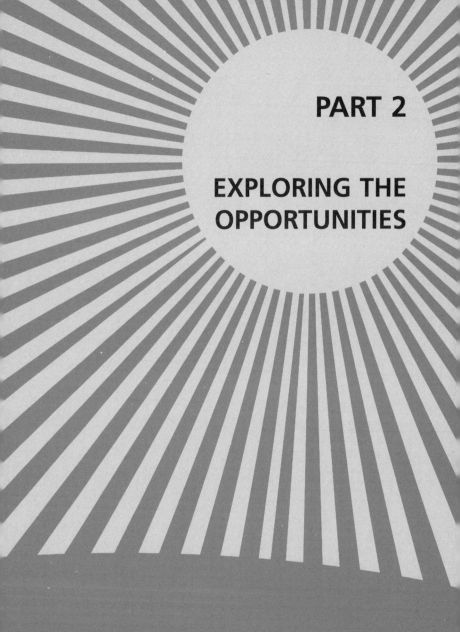

PART 2

EXPLORING THE OPPORTUNITIES

Now we have made the case for self-employment and understand the opportunities that are opening up before us, we need to explore where to start and what to watch out for along the way.

CHAPTER 9

FACE THE FACTS BEFORE YOU START

. . . In which we discover how hard it is to get an honest opinion of our plans and how vitally important it is to face up to reality.

HONESTY

As we plan our enterprise and decide what it is we want to do, the one thing we need, and which is almost impossible to find, is honesty. I don't mean our honesty as it relates to our integrity with customers, suppliers, or even the law. What I am referring to is the honesty – the brutal, tough, uncompromising honesty – that we are going to need from others about our enterprise so that we avoid the horrible fate that awaits the deluded when it comes to self-employment.

How will you find out if your ideas are sound before you sink your life savings into them (first tip, don't sink your life savings into them)? Perhaps you could ask me my honest opinion, but even then you might not get it. The thing is that I am writing this book with a picture of you in my mind, and I desperately want you to succeed through the tips or even, dare I say it, the inspiration that the book gives you. But I also want to be loved, so when you ask me what I think of your idea I find it impossibly hard to tell you that it is crap.

Beauty is not in the eye of the beholder

I was watching a business guru the other day – I think he had been one of the Dragons from 'Dragons' Den'. He summed up the situation beautifully by calling it, 'The ugly baby syndrome'. The idea is that you meet an old friend carrying their new baby. They show it proudly to you. To your horror, you notice that this thing is so ugly that it could stop a clock. What is your reaction, what do you say? Do you say, "My heavens, he's an ugly little brute and no mistake!" I bet you don't. You say something like, "He's a tough little guy. I bet he is going to be a football player when he grows up."

This ugly baby thing really got me thinking, because there is a lot to it if you can relate your infant enterprise to the concept of the ugly baby. First, can you ever see your own baby as ugly? They say children are like farts, you can just about tolerate your own. Perhaps the same applies to enterprises.

Consider the 'footballer' comment that people made when looking at the baby; it is quite clear that there is a clue to our beloved's challenges in the looks department. I notice that if I don't want to upset, I use weasel words like, "Perhaps you could try . . . ", "It is bright and cheerful but what about a more subdued range for your less adventurous customers . . . ". The problem is that we don't actually want to hear anything bad about our ideas but we do need to – weasel words and equivocal comments are clues but they are only clues if we have the courage to look for them. I could suggest that we are irrevocably blinded to our offspring's failings and, dare I say it, similarly blinded to the shortcomings of our ideas.

Would I lie to you?

I am billed as the world's toughest business guru, the Hell's Angel of management consultancy, and have the appearance of a night-club doorman . . . Well, if that is the case and even I am intimidated by your heartbreak, what chance have you got?

Take your own situation. It may well be that you have joined some kind of start-up group, or you have discussed ideas with friends. I regularly speak to groups like this and there is always some lunatic who has the most bizarre idea from the Planet Zarg – something like teaching dogs to weld. I earwig in during the coffee breaks and hear you, yes you, telling this idiot that this is a great idea. "So you can teach dogs to weld?"

"I believe I can!" says this maniac, fixing you with the gaze of a true fanatic. "Do you own a dog?"

"I have a poodle."

"They would make excellent welders; it's the woolly coat, you see, resistant to conflagration from stray sparks. You are a very lucky person; you have a true potential canine welder. Perhaps when I set up I should come and see you."

Your reply – is it a cry of derision? A sharp slap-down? No! You say, "That would be great. Toto a welder, hey? Well I never."

When I go around the group and am told of the plan for welding dogs, instead of hurling this genius into the stormy night all I can manage is, "What makes you think there is a call for welding dogs? Have you done any research?" Of course he has, everyone he asks has welcomed the idea, even you. With assurance he sets up 'Bark Welding', then one day there is a knock at your door and there he stands, laden down with gas bottles and miniature goggles. It is time for Toto's first foray into the fiery art of bonding metals. Well it's your own fault, you encouraged him.

REALITY TELEVISION

I was approached by BBC Television to do a business rescue reality show called 'All Over the Shop'. The idea was that I would visit small, one-person enterprises that were struggling, and with the power of genius and perspicacity I would set them straight. The problem was that I wasn't that confident that I was a perspicacious genius.

"Don't worry," said the producer. "This is TV. We can work magic; we can even make you look intelligent and engaged."

The strange thing is that the show, despite being agonizingly low budget, was quite a hit, and even more astonishing was the fact that nearly all the businesses became roaring successes. Was this down to my genius or ability as a business guru? I doubt it but, believe it or not, I think it was about honesty.

The TV researchers are genuinely brilliant; when you watch reality shows and say, "Where on earth do they find these people?" it is the result of hours of painstaking work by the researchers. They are looking for characters and, let me tell you, they found me some real corkers – people who made welding dogs seem pedestrian and mainstream. The researchers knew everything about the enterprise I was visiting but they rationed the information they gave to me. We would arrive in a truck with a director, runners, a film crew and a sound technician. I would be given some sparse but provocative clues, such as, "Ask her about where she got her loan" or "Ask him when he last drew a wage". They knew the reply would be something sinister and wanted to see the sparks fly. Then I would be cast from the truck to go and sort things out. The show was well received and got mostly good reviews from the press, but one critic who hated it said probably the most honest thing about it. The review said, "Geoff Burch wanders in, states the bleedin' obvious and then wanders out again. Then four weeks later everything has miraculously changed for the better and all is well." That is, in fact, exactly what did happen but we need to understand why.

Tough talk

On the first day of the first shoot I ambled into the first enterprise and met lovely but barking mad people who were making a complete pig's ear of things.

"Well, it all looks very nice," I said.

Our director was a small fiery Welsh woman with a ferocious temper. She leapt forward, grabbed my ear and dragged me outside for a savage talking-to.

"Very nice? VERY NICE?!" she stamped like Rumplestiltskin. "This is telly. I want you to tear them to bits, Mr Tough Business Guru."

"I don't like to, they're nice."

"Listen, mush, that is the deal. Their businesses will be seen by millions of viewers, they want to be on the telly. This is the price they will have to pay. You are here to entertain the viewers, that is what you are paid for. You are not here as a business consultant, you are here to entertain. These enterprises are not your customers, the viewers are, and they want to see you give it to them right between the eyes, car crash TV. So remember . . ." she put her hands up in the shape of tiger claws, "grrr, grrr, grrr, grrr!"

So that's what I did. If their food was horrible, I told them. If the shop looked rough, I told them. If they were untidy or unprofessional, I told them. If I ever held back my eye would catch on to this small, vigorous figure behind the camera jumping up and down, hands like claws and silently mouthing, "Grrr, grrr, grrr!"

Take it on the chin

On the other side of this equation, the people in the enterprises took it. Sure, there were huge rows, shouting and tears, but they stood and took it because they were on TV. They took it on board, they changed and they became successful. It is not my skill, this happens in every TV reality show – 'Kitchen Nightmares', 'Mary Queen of Shops', 'Hotel Inspector', you name them, they all bring success. Why? Because in the real world you would never get such honesty about your enterprise. You may believe that the success was down to the exposure to millions of viewers, but the whole show is in the can before anyone sees it. In my own case, it was over a year before it went to air, so the business transformation was caused by the enterprises meeting the horrible truth fair and square. The problem for us is, without the aid of TV how can we get this honest appraisal of our position?

A matter of taste

A dear friend of ours produces custom-made corporate chocolates. He has come from a marketing background so he knows his onions as far as that's concerned, and what he has done is to invest in a very clever printer that works with edible inks. This means that chocolates can be created with a company's logo or pictures on them. This enterprise took off a storm but soon started to peter out, but why? We ordered some of these chocolates for a special celebration and we discovered why things weren't going too well. The chocolate tasted horrible – well actually not horrible, it was worse than that, it tasted a bit like dog treats. Now, you would think that this fault was blindingly obvious but while everyone could see it, no one dared mention it.

THE MORAL OF THE STORY

The famous question, "Does my bum look big in this?" will never elicit an honest answer.

Tom Peters tells a wonderful story of a huge American corporation that decided to go into the dog food business. Their mighty marketing department chose special colours for the packaging that their research had told them particularly appealed to dog owners. The psychology department said that the size of the can gave certain perceptions of quality. The logistics department made sure every store on the continent possessed sufficient stock. The project cost millions and was supposed to buy the dog food market, but the results were horribly disappointing. The CEO gathered a huge contingent of the team together and addressed them.

"We spent millions, the packaging is great, the distribution is great, the marketing is great; what went wrong?"

From the back of the hall, from the darkest corner, an anonymous voice called back, "The dogs hate it!"

TOO NICE

So how are we going to set this vital honesty in place in our enterprise before we have a disaster? Before we get started in our enterprise, we don't just have to face some truths, but we have to find those truths first. Let's take our chocolate maker: if no one will tell us what is wrong, how do we find out? Firstly, let's understand why no one will tell us the truth. It is just too tough to tell someone you know right to their face that they have made a mistake. I was going to say that it is because people are too nice to be hurtful but then I realized that people do sometimes indulge in a bit of back-stabbing which reveals the truth as they see it but is never given to us face to face.

"Did you see the state of her?"

"We know their Brian is up to all sorts but they are too blind to see it."

"If Gary carries on like that he is going to get fired."

Well, why not warn Gary? Because you may feel it is a very dangerous move and Gary won't thank you or even feel grateful.

My father, who was possessed of that wonderfully dismal Eastern European view of the world, used to quote a Russian proverb which said, "When the squires agree, the peasant gets his arse kicked" – a warning to anyone who wishes to intercede between two people on a collision course. So we can backstab and gossip but can't be truthful to each other's face. The answer then is to pretend not to be you . . .

Finding the hidden truth

Imagine you are in the bar with chums. Instead of saying, "I'm thinking of teaching dogs to weld", say, with a dismissive chuckle, "What do you think of a person who wants to teach dogs to weld?"

More sensibly, if you were the chocolate maker, I would suggest that you don a brightly coloured acrylic blazer and a stupid cheap clip-on bow tie, and go out into the world as an independent researcher as can be seen on every main street and shopping mall the world over. Carry a tray with Hershey bars, Cadbury's chocolates, Lindt, and your own. "Would you like to take the chocolate test?" If the public say without actually knowing who you are that your product is horrible, then it is horrible. If they score you tenth out of ten, then you need to do something about it.

Only the best is good enough?

Actually, in such a survey I wouldn't be that happy to be even second out of ten because there would always be a competitor who offered a tastier alternative. Hurry back and consider that statement very carefully because from this moment on we need to make a living from this.

Let's examine the position. What proposition will you make to the customer (this is the person that pays us for our effort, remember).

"Buy my chocolate, accepted universally as being second best." As a customer, surely I would want to buy the best chocolate. So what incentive can you offer me to get me to buy the second best chocolate? There is a very strong philosophical point to make here and it is one that you have to consider before we move on together. The question is, how near to the best do you need or want to get? If you remember from earlier on, we discussed the formulae of value = benefit − cost. The temptation of the self-employed is to take the mindset of "Because it's just me, I can do it cheaper". This would fit the formula, "Good value = dodgy benefit − little cost" but as we saw with the amateur surgeon, in some cases the risk is just too great and does not represent good value at all, so is simply scary.

Our corporate chocolate maker may get away with this, however, because to have the greatest chocolate in the world was not his unique business proposition. The deal is that you can have a choccy bar with your logo on, or your happy smiling face leering back at you off it! As long as it tastes good up to main street candy store standards, you are OK, and at risk of shooting myself in the foot here, you can go too far "Oh yes, our cocoa beans are the only ones that have been through the digestive tract of the rare mountain lemur!" "But will it say Sid's Garage clearly on each bar?"

The conclusion we must draw from all of this is that of course it is vitally important to get the truth about our enterprise but it is equally important, when we have got that truth, to do something about it. By acting as a researcher or independent adviser we can stand away from our own enterprise and look at it objectively and with other eyes. Even if the answers we get are disappointing or worrying, don't pack them away and try to ignore or forget about them, do something about it.

POINTS TO PONDER ON
'FACE THE FACTS BEFORE WE START'

- It's very hard to get the truth about your ideas. No one will tell you if you've got an ugly baby or an ugly enterprise.

- People who love or like you would never hurt you by telling you the truth . . . come to think of it, nor will strangers either.

- If you don't feature in a reality TV show you'll have to find another way of getting an honest appraisal of your ideas.

- Get out on the street and pretend to be an independent market researcher to get some real honesty.

- If someone tells you they can teach your dog to weld and you tell them they are a genius, you are not doing them any favours.

- If someone tells you you are a genius, they are not doing you any favours either.

CHAPTER 10

WHY WOULD YOU WANT TO DO THAT?

. . . In which we realize we have to be different in order to stand head and shoulders above the competition, and we investigate the magic arithmetic that tells us we either succeed or fail.

ANOTHER GIFT SHOP

As we choose our enterprise, our offer must be considered and precise for our intended market. In my experience, many self-employed start ups don't have much use for any of the words in that statement – not considered, not precise, not even intended, and no idea of the market.

I love the expression, 'Ready, Fire, Aim' – it just about sums it up. A comedian once ruminated on the origin of egg consumption; what prompted early *Homo sapiens* to watch a bird produce an egg from where it produces eggs and think to themselves, "I'm going to try and eat that!" I have just the same sense of wonder when I see what enterprises people have chosen.

There is an enterprise paradox; if there aren't any competitors it is probably because it is impossible to make money. If there are lots of competitors, how is the newcomer supposed to survive against them?

WHAT THIS PLACE NEEDS IS . . .

During the filming of my TV show, 'All Over the Shop', one of my most infamous tirades was aimed at a gift shop. The people who ran it were lovely but a bit bewildered. The clip, which I think is still on the internet, shows me frothing at the mouth and shouting, "A gift shop, I bet that was well considered! Who on earth thinks things through and says to themselves, what this town needs is another gift shop?!"

More coffee shops than people

I live in a modest sized town and yet a recent survey found that there were 250 separate establishments where you could buy a cup of coffee, including of course MacDonald's, Starbucks, Caffè Nero and Costa Coffee. So what is it I see opening every day? Why a coffee shop, of course.

OK, here is an exercise for you. Against all advice, your mad Uncle Harry has put the entire family fortune up against a start-up coffee shop and then done a bunk. The family prevails upon you to be the saviour of their fortunes, so despite your better judgement and the advice of this book, you find yourself running your coffee shop in a small town with 250 competitors. How are you going to pull this one off? The choice you have is around the offer you make to your customers and the activity – or dare I say aggression – with which you promote it.

So begin with the offer you are going to make. Maybe the cheapest cup of coffee in town? That is a route that I hate and would always advise against, but OK, let's see how it would work.

First, you have to understand that you are playing a very tough game that attracts some very tough and professional players. One of the things that I bang on and on about is professionalism, and a lot of people believe that if their offer is based on the lowest price model that somehow they can compromise professionalism. This is just not the case: people like Poundland, 99 Cents Store, and Ryanair are extremely professional – you have to be to run at such tight margins.

Well, OK then, you may feel that cheapest is dodgy but 'best' and 'most expensive' may be a step too far the other way. Perhaps we could stodge around in the middle somewhere which is where all the other independent coffee shops seem to lurk.

So if not price, what other offer can you make your customers? The point is that people start their enterprises, often convinced of their ability, often assured of their skill, but what they do fail to do is to put themselves into the mind of their potential customer and ask why they should be chosen against the competition. Once, salespeople used to be obsessed with a thing they called the USP or unique sales proposition, the thing that set them aside from any competition that they were up against. Just reflect for a moment, what is your USP – without one, you are doomed. Remember, you never see just one lemming! Whether it is your location, your price, your quality, or the fact that you wander around stark naked apart from a pair of socks, there must be something that makes you remarkable, different and head and shoulders above the rest – in one aspect, at least.

Needs must

In order to make your offer fully considered you also need to look at your catchment area of business. For a coffee shop this may mean your town. If your enterprise is, for example, business intelligence, then you should consider the whole country is your catchment area. If you manufacture strange aircraft parts, the whole world can be in your catchment area. OK, why does this town need another coffee shop when there are already 250? What is it that people are thinking? Remember the knobbly stick threat for anyone who says, "What this place needs is a . . .". How do you know that it is what this place needs – whether it's coffee shop, accountant, beauty therapist, hairdresser, or goat breeder? Do your research and make sure you actually know what this place needs and you haven't just assumed you know.

It doesn't add up

I have a friend who . . . well, I was going to say runs a gardening business, but what he actually does is do a bit of gardening for people who pay him, and very happy he is with this, too. I asked him, "If you didn't do gardening, what enterprise would you start? The reply was, "Well, there is absolutely nowhere to get a mower or a hedge trimmer fixed for miles around here." He had identified a demand, therefore surely he was then entitled to utter the fatal words, "What this place needs is someone who can fix garden machinery . . . hey, what's with the knobbly stick, Geoff?"

What had he done wrong? Surely he had identified a need, but had he? Just because there isn't one doesn't mean the world needs one. Just for a moment, bear with me while we do a few sums.

At the time of writing this I have broken my tumble dryer. I have deduced from hours of fiddling that it is the timer, the cost of which is £50 and the tumble dryer cost £150 new. If I were a tumble dryer repairman, I would have to charge for a few hours work, my travelling and the part, which I estimate to be marginally more than the price of a new tumble dryer. The same applies to garden machinery – a Chinese made motor mower can be had for £100. Why would you ever bother fixing it at £20 or £30 an hour plus spares? If this is the enterprise you are considering starting, you may know more than me because this is just off the top of my head stuff, but then I am not betting my future prosperity on it. You might be.

The point I am trying to make is that as well as deciding what offer you are going to make to persuade your customers to buy from you over your competition, you also need to have done your sums and be as sure as possible that there is some element of viability before plunging in.

Optimistic arithmetic

We have barely dipped one tiny toe in the chilly waters of self-employment and yet already we can see why so many enterprises fail or are doomed before they even get started. First, they haven't done the simplest of maths – I don't mean business plans or cash flow forecasts either (they remind me too much of blackcurrant picking, anyway). No, I mean the really simple stuff.

This simple maths is particularly important when starting up an enterprise where there are none already.

On one of my courses I had a guy who told me that he wasn't really interested in what I said because he was a genius on the verge of making millions and he was only there so that he could become eligible for certain government grants. What was his secret, I asked, and he told me that he had invented a very simple device that could be fitted to a shower that would halve water costs. It was indeed brilliant and simple and if you saw one you would see how it worked and with a pair of scissors and a plastic shopping bag you could make your own. He knew this and was going to sell them for just a few pence each and, being plastic, they would last forever. "How much do you think my company will turn over?" he asked smugly. "About a million," I replied. "What's that, a day, a week, a month?" he asked. "No," I said, "altogether before it has to shut down." "Don't be stupid," he said. "The investment in manufacture alone will be a couple of million." I explained that our water system is unique so the rest of the world couldn't benefit and that at a rough estimate there were about 10 million showers here. So if everyone had one of his products (100% penetration) at 10 pence each, he might turn over one million and then pack up. He wouldn't, or couldn't, believe me, and in the event the outcome was even worse because very few people could be bothered to fiddle about with their showers anyway and it all ended in tears.

NO VACANCIES

Setting up a self-employed enterprise, whether a coffee shop or as an independent accountant or executive counsellor, is all about job vacancies. In the world of employment, you would only get a job if there was a vacancy – no accountants needed, no vacancies. Now you are self-employed, your employer is you.

In the traditional job market it is very simple and straightforward. When a commercial employer finds that a certain task cannot be done by their current complement of people, they must search for a further person to undertake that identified task. Therefore, there is a vacancy, a gap that needs filling, a job that needs to be done. In other words, work is, remember, the effort that someone is prepared to pay us to undertake. What makes life even easier is that the prospective employer has priced this work with a fixed sum called a wage. The choice for you is stark: take it or leave it. If there is one job vacancy and thirty applicants, by some arcane and arbitrary form of selection, one person is offered the job and twenty nine don't get it. That person gets all the work and all the money, what there is of it.

Imagine, though, that this vacancy might or might not guarantee paid work, and if it did, the other twenty nine applicants could still fight you for the honour of doing it – and what if the victor didn't corner the market but had to share it with the others on an entirely random and unfair basis? Well, not to be too dismal, that is self-employment. The rewards financially and psychologically are huge but this is the price we have to pay.

Remember when you start your enterprise, there is no job vacancy – you will be creating one out of thin air and that may take some guts. It is like showing up at your local supermarket and starting to serve the customers. It wouldn't be long before the staff notice and say, "Oi, this is my job", to which you reply, "Tough! I work faster, harder, better. Let the customers decide who to do business with." Outrageous, perhaps, but that is exactly what happens when you start an enterprise. You create an enterprise by shouldering everyone else to one side.

Perhaps you have a unique idea that no other person on the planet has tried before (like welding dogs). Whilst that has huge dangers of its own, you will still be competing for cash that would have otherwise been spent in a more traditional area. Therefore we are all in the competition business one way or the other.

Well, you're the boss

So if your new employer is going to be you, the first question to be asked of this employer is, is there a vacancy? What have you chosen to be your enterprise? Skills training, hairdressing, management counselling, or yes, I suppose a shop or a coffee shop (online or otherwise)? Assuming that there are other people already doing it in the catchment area we have marked out, to make room for us in this area we are going to have to shoulder someone out of the way or pick up the expansion in their expanding market that they were looking forward to getting. This, in a way, is a pretty aggressive attitude and, whilst I don't want you scampering about with a switchblade and a pair of knuckle dusters, you must be prepared to be, shall we say, fairly proactive when it comes to finding a seat for you and your family in this world's precarious lifeboat.

Boxing clever

Closer to home, one of my sons, who was tiring of his high powered city job and whose passion is boxing, asked me if I would help him to find a boxing and fitness gym to run. He said that this new relaxed lifestyle would be enhanced with a bit of sunshine so we set off to southern Spain to view gyms for sale. Buying an established enterprise can sometimes be the way to go but with some thumping great big caveats. The first thing to consider is why the enterprise is being sold. The reasons are many and varied – retirement, ill health, a desire to try something different, marriage break-up, a failure of a partnership, the offer of a great job elsewhere, or even the overwhelming success of their other enterprises means that they just do not have enough time for the one they are selling. Most of the above should be taken with a pinch of salt and in a lot of cases are not true. Again, to repeat the message of this chapter, it is all about doing your sums. Whether you are starting an enterprise or buying an enterprise, don't listen to your heart, the seller's apparent explanations, but look at the figures, decide how much you need to live, and if the sums don't add up just walk away. It is as simple as that.

Mother knows best

However, by doing just that my Mum made her living. I remember that with a stubby pencil and the back of one of her cigarette packets, she would create a column of figures that in seconds would tell her whether the proposition was good or bad.

My mother would buy other people's enterprises and turn them into gold mines before selling them on at a profit. She was never fooled by stories, she could see if a business was underperforming, but, more importantly, she could see potential. Out of twenty or thirty businesses for sale that I was dragged around to see as a kid, only one would get that glint in her eye. Bear in mind that, although she was a dear old Mum to me, in the real world she was a ruthless, precise and skilful retailer, who had trained for years in the big London department stores from shop floor to buyer. I remember once she bought a general store and she was stamping about saying, "Bloody gripe water! Who on earth orders eight cases of bloody gripe water!" The previous owners were new at the game and their stocking policy tended to be guided by the powers of influence of the company salespeople who visited. I remember the sales guys waiting to see Mum physically trembling with anxiety and with good reason! (By the way, everyone who shopped there for weeks afterwards were offered the incredible opportunity of owning a miraculous bottle of gripe water that did oh so many things other than settle a child's stomach! It did everything from cleaning furniture to soothing piles.) If you touched the outside of one of my Mum's shops it seemed to hum like a generating station with the energy of what went on inside. Could you do that? Could you be sure you have seen the potential? Could you, through ceaseless energy, do so much better than the current owner? If you aren't sure, don't do it.

Not as good as it looked

Going back to my son's situation, he and I set off for Spain which was in the grip of a financial meltdown. This meant enterprises were cheap – a good thing – but also meant that everyone was broke, which is a bad thing. We narrowed our viewings down to three gyms with potential. They seemed to be ticking along, were a bit rundown, and the owners had just seemed to lose heart. With a bit of energy, things could have been perfect and my son became quite enthusiastic. One place had two hundred regular members who paid 30 Euros a month each, which is 6000 Euros a month coming in. "That's not bad," my son said. I pointed out that after rent, power, repairs and wages, he would be left with less than 12,000 Euros a year. I had done that vital arithmetic and realized that the idea was a non-starter. He accused me of 'pissing on his parade' but later was very relieved that he hadn't gone ahead with this scheme for all sorts of reasons.

POINTS TO PONDER ON
'WHY WOULD YOU WANT TO DO THAT?'

- Be aware of the risks of choosing an enterprise in a market that is flooded with enterprises similar to your own.

- If you do, what is it about your enterprise that makes everyone choose you above the competition?

- When choosing your enterprise, don't guess the need, prove the need.

- Although it is disappointing to find the sums don't add up, it's better to find out now than crash and burn later.

- If the sums don't add up, it is clever to just walk away.

- With self-employment, we create our own vacancy and may need to make our own space.

- You can buy a failing enterprise if your arithmetic suggests you can do better than the previous people, but you had better be right.

- Do you have a detailed report on your potential customers, a forensic analysis of at least ten of your closest competitors and an independent, frank, unbiased opinion of your offering?

CHAPTER **11**

JUST THE JOB

. . . In which we consider what job we are going to give ourselves, why we shouldn't give ourselves a job we are likely to get bored with, and discover what motivates people to choose us.

THE SELECTION PROCESS

The next question we need to ask is, what job are you actually giving yourself? There is a whole industry built around the so-called science of personnel selection – in other words, getting the right person for the right job. Inside big companies, a huge amount of time and money is swallowed up by the human resources department, which I find strange as they never seem very human or very resourceful. These people also spend even more money on external resources such as psychometric testing and recruitment consultants. I think it is mostly mumbo jumbo and cant but there must be a tiny grain of reality in what they are trying to do. Jobs are currently hard to find so when a reasonable one comes along there will be a queue of eager people wanting to do it.

The first step is to send in a CV or a résumé. Something in that causes a great number of applicants to be rejected. What was it that HR saw? A lot of people get their CV or résumé professionally written by people who know what they are doing, but still get rejected at that first hurdle. Why is that? Too old, too young, some sort of prejudice against them, underqualified, overqualified, too many previous jobs, too few previous jobs? While HR people are not my favourite folk, previous experience must have told them something. If they are considering employing someone, there will be certain circumstances and disqualifying factors that will lead them to not choose certain applicants. These could be anything from experience, ability and, even though it is illegal, they may also privately take into account ethnicity, disability and age. I am sure they would deny this, but the point I am trying to make is that in self-employment we will be providing our own job regardless of any factor that may restrict our ability to do that job. We are going to give the job to ourselves that we have created for ourselves, but we must also be fully aware of the consequences of giving ourselves a job that may be perceived as inappropriate to our skills and personality by an outside judge. It is also worth bearing in mind that an HR department will recruit as to need, vacancies, and the number of people required. Again, the self-employed tend to give themselves a job even when there isn't a vacancy and the quantity of work goes to the person with the sharpest elbows.

A qualified decision

The job that you have planned for yourself in the self-employment world is one that I am sure you will give to yourself, but in the mind of that HR person what is the consequence of giving the job to the wrong person? Say you are one of the lucky few who gets a job interview, during which you are told the classic cliché that you are 'overqualified'. What on earth does that mean, how can anybody be overqualified? Surely, it would be good to employ someone overqualified; they could do the job standing on their head. Just for a moment put yourself into the mind of that HR person and try and argue their case for a minute. Have a think and imagine you are in HR and tell me as many reasons as you can why you shouldn't employ someone you consider to be overqualified. I can imagine that they may become bored if their mind is not fully occupied and challenged, but so what, most people are bored with proper jobs or they wouldn't be reading books like this. The trouble with bored people is that they either stay and become disruptive, they try to expand the job into uncharted and dangerous waters, or they up and leave.

The coffee rickshaw

Now let's have a bit of a think about the job you are going to give yourself and how it fits your CV. You may be tired of the frantic rat race that is city derivatives trading, sick of the challenges of brain surgery, or the cut and thrust of defence at the High Court. What you crave is a little peace of mind, perhaps a peddle rickshaw that pulls a real coffee machine out there in the dappled sunlight that streams through the trees, enjoying good fresh air and exercise as you peddle through the mellow streets dispensing REAL coffee to all who want it. Can I just pop that bubble a bit by suggesting you could be a teeny weeny bit overqualified for this one. When it is pissing with rain and you are peddling this cursed contraption up some bleak hill, will you remember your nice warm office, the company car and the free lunches?

The problem is that, although I just conjured this idea out of my head, enterprises such as this actually do quite well; nice and simple, a good cup of real coffee brought to you. What happens is that over time you build up a loyal following of people who will wait for your arrival come rain or sunshine. It will build up to a nice little earner, a few yummy extras can be added like the odd cookie or doughnut, but that is about it. How long are you going to keep that up? Let's imagine that 'Coffee by Rickshaw' earns enough to provide what even you may describe as a very good standard of living. Will you be pedalling for two years, ten years, twenty years, or even forty? Oh, ten, is it? For ten long years you pedal this thing – and then what? You sell it? You set fire to it? You expand and buy fifty of the things and become a rickshaw baron? You realize that you have a formula for a nice gentle money spinning idea and franchise it?

I am not saying that a manual job is undesirable – actually fixing things like cars or washing machines, or making things like dresses or houses is surprisingly mentally challenging and also very stimulating. All I am saying is go into this thing with your eyes wide open and understand exactly what job you are giving yourself. It is going to be no use whatsoever if you are going to get bored and disruptive or feel trapped by the conflict between a steady income stream and turgid repetitive work. That is, after all, what you are trying to get away from . . . it is called having a job!

SEE THE TROUBLE COMING

The solution to these problems is preparation, which is the last thing most self-employed people indulge in. People accuse me (with some justification, to be fair) of being a pessimist, but in my defence I would say I was an adventurous (or foolhardy) pessimist. Would I, for the right money or incentive, sail a yacht across the Atlantic single handed? For me, that would be a terrifying and lonely business and to get me to do it the rewards would have to be huge. The questions to ask before setting out are, how dangerous is this? How many people have failed before? What were the consequences? The answers, in that order are, very, loads, and some were never seen again! The other side of that coin is that loads of people have succeeded. If we examine the successes and the failures, a large batch of both could put their fate down to sheer luck. Good or bad, I am eager for this book to remove luck as a necessary element of our enterprise. The ones who arrive despite being incompetent sailors in leaky ill-equipped boats are just playing a damp sort of Russian roulette, and the apparently well sorted ones who sink through 'bad luck' usually have some feature of what they did that contributed to their demise. Maybe they were experienced, perhaps the boat was state of the art, but because they were pushing hard everything was under too much strain. My choice – and remember this is my choice, for you will have your own choices to make which is the fun and joy of self determination – would be to have a very well prepared boat, sailed well within my and its capability. I would be well versed in the dangers and obstacles before I set off, my arrival would be inevitable – timings and route may change, but I would get there. Let's apply that inevitability to our enterprise.

Did you think it through?

Sorry about this, but I'm going to get back to the coffee shop again. I'm not suggesting that you should consider a coffee shop but it is iconic of the mindset of the ill-considered enterprise. Dressmaking, taxi driving, teaching piano, servicing cars, mending washing machines, window cleaning, nuclear physics, management training or whatever, the rules are the same for this exercise so for now it's coffee shop. You must travel with me into the mind of our subject, a senior purchasing manager for an industrial conglomerate. The thunderbolt of redundancy strikes, leaving a lump sum and no gainful employment "Hey, let's open a coffee shop." Why? What was the logic behind that? Is there a vacancy? Does he realize what job he is about to give himself? Consider this, whatever enterprise you choose will require you to do work – that work is the job that you will be giving yourself. The choice of enterprise will be irrevocably linked to the type of effort you will have to expend during your working day. Remember, in the old world of wage slavery we would not be offered our shackles until a previous rower had failed and been thrown over the side. There was no job until there was a vacancy, and once we had been through the interview process to determine whether we were under- or overqualified, we might have been offered the vacant job. At that point, there would be an empty chair to fill and we wouldn't have to fight for it. Because we are not used to fighting for our work, I suppose that is why we might turn a blind eye to the competition when choosing our enterprise, but also remember this paradox: if no one is doing it, it's probably a bad idea; if it is a good idea, probably loads of people are already doing it. Worse than this in the case of coffee shops, loads of people are doing it and I am still not convinced that it is a good idea.

The secret of their success

You are determined to open a coffee shop so let's make it work. First, visit a minimum of ten competitors; chat up the staff or the owner or anyone who will talk. Try not to tell them your plans; we need a bit of sneaky here. Are they making money? What makes them the most money? Do they feel their position (geographical) is affecting their business? What sort of cup or mugs do they use, what food offering do they have? Don't just visit them once but also on weekends, midweek, wet days, sunny days, evening and morning. Do the sums, watch the customers and notice how long they are staying and how much they spend. For instance, the coffee shop is packed (hoorah), and that's about thirty people for the peak three hours of the day. For the rest of the day they average around ten customers. A cup of coffee gives a gross profit of £1.00 so that is £90 earned in the peak and £50 for the rest of the day – so £140 per day. Well, busy or not, that won't pay the rent. You could make more driving a bus. Remember, if you have a proper job you will be paid a wage. Because of this, employed people lose the connection between the money they receive and the job that they do. For the self-employed, the choice of enterprise and the profit it makes relate exactly to the money we take home. In other words, the profit is our wage – no profit, no wage.

OK, in your research group you find some little gold mines. What makes them special? Is it the food, is it the position, or the quality of what they offer? Dress up in your market research outfit again and interview their customers. So, you have found the good ones; how are you going to push them to one side and how will you take away their customers? Why will people choose you?

Judge by appearance

It always astonishes me when I walk into any enterprise where the people involved cannot see that their appearance and behaviour affect their financial performance.

I bet this is a familiar scene. You walk into a tatty shop in a secondary shopping area to see a damp nosed girl with a cardigan pulled over her hands, crouching over a portable gas heater and eating a pot noodle. Doomed! Inevitably doomed! It's the same with twee names – a hairdresser called 'Curl Up and Dye' may survive but you would never see it in the West End of London or in Manhattan. What you are like and what you do will put certain limits on you. A good test is to be blindfolded and be led into a small, independent enterprise or a national (or even internationally) renowned one. When the blindfold is removed it will, without seeing any signage, be clear who the independent is. The deep fascination for me while researching this book is how people, individual people, achieve value. The big mistake individual self-employed people make is to feel that one of their few unique selling points is the ability to be cheap. Is that the way Beethoven thought? "Listen mate, 'cause it's just me working alone I will knock you up a symphony cheap!" Does Warren Buffett give you a bit of cheap financial advice? Will Raymond Blanc do your daughter's wedding food because it's just him working alone? Actually, he would probably be delighted to do your daughter's wedding personally if you are prepared to pay him a few hundred pounds per head. His reasons for charging such eye watering amounts? "Because I shall be working on this alone", the very reason why you think it would be a good idea to be cheap. What's your answer to this . . . because he's famous? Then get famous. Because he is brilliant? Then get brilliant. Because he is famous for being brilliant? Then become so brilliant that you become famous.

You would not expect to be offered a job by walking into a prospective employer and saying, "Can I have the job, I'll do it cheaper." So why do so many people believe that it will work when we become self-employed? To clarify this, we have to see that our customers are our employers and they will give us our work based on the quality of our offer, not the price of it. When we go for a job, we go to our prospective employer dressed in our Sunday best and on our very best behaviour, in other words we try and sell ourselves to our employer. We should adopt exactly the same attitude whenever we come into contact with a prospective customer. Each and every contact is a job interview; tatty, bored, dishevelled and unprofessional, does not get us the job.

POINTS TO PONDER ON 'JUST THE JOB'

- When you plan your enterprise, understand what job you are actually giving yourself.

- What are the consequences of giving yourself a job that you are going to get bored with?

- Don't let the dangers stop you but be aware of them so that you can plan ahead.

- Although it may be disappointing, when you give yourself a job interview for your planned enterprise, if you discover that you really are not qualified for the job, perhaps you should consider not doing it.

- Understand that the criteria used in job selection could be applied by your customers to select or deselect you.

- The way you look directly affects the value of your enterprise because that is how your customers will qualify you. Why would you ever choose to behave in a manner that will reduce your perceived value?

CHAPTER 12

THE FAME GAME

. . . In which we build the value of our name and see the benefit of doing things the way the true professionals do it.

THE NAME IS THE GAME

We are on a journey at the end of which hopefully we will be in possession of something that is of improved value. In the world of commerce, the thing that everyone wants to end up with is a valuable brand. For the self-employed, may I suggest that we aim for a similar goal, but in our case that thing of value, our brand, should be our name. I would suggest that this is preferably our own name; I have absolutely no idea why the self-employed choose a name for their enterprise that isn't their own. What are you trying to hide? The thing that really winds me up is the 'twee' name. Seriously, what do you think having a twee name will achieve? Where have you seen a twee name succeed (I suppose they do sometimes but on the whole in the real world success and fame tend to tie to a real name). Here is a list . . . Ford, Sears, Marks & Spencer, Cadbury, Kellogg's, Barry

Manilow, Barclays, Carnegie, and on and on it goes. In any high street or stock exchange, so many enterprises carry the name of the founder. Are you shy, or perhaps ashamed of your name? The other great advantage of using your own name against a twee one is that it gives you flexibility. If you start as 'The Coffee Table Workshop', then for the rest of time you will make coffee tables, but if you are 'Gladys Prong Designs' you may find wooden toys prove more lucrative than coffee tables with no change of name needed.

Next, if you look at that list of names they are successes each and every one. Why? Because they are, or were, brilliant individuals. Does that daunt you? Why? Are you planning to be crap? "No, Geoff, I will become crap by accident!" You have been into crap coffee shops, rubbish enterprises; you have been driven wild by unreliable builders, sent insane by vague mechanics, frightened by apparently inept business advisors. You've seen it and yet you fear you might go the same way. Look, you have seen the bad, under-confident, the unprofessional, you recognize it, you acknowledge it, so DON'T DO IT.

This section of the book is about becoming well known but, of course, you have to become well known for being good. An awful lot of small enterprises are very well known for being bad! I recently had cause to do business with a small motorcycle repair workshop. The guy did a good job and charged a reasonable price, but on the internet the comments against him were horrendous and he was described as surly and unhelpful. The first point is that he didn't even know these reviews were out there and, secondly, he didn't feel it was important to do anything about them. With the world the way it is, as soon as you do anything bad, everyone gets to hear about it and your reputation can go global. Make sure you have a reputation for being reliable, good value, helpful and professional.

FAMOUS

Famous is another key word. You absolutely and utterly need to be famous but only in the catchment area of your customers. If you are a window cleaner, get famous in ten streets. If you are a hairdresser, maybe the whole town should have heard of you. Are you a collector and distributor of rare and weird insects? Then tell the world.

Positioning

Don't think from this that I am suggesting that you become the most expensive, or that you should battle your way ruthlessly towards that top slot. What I am talking about is what the marketing men call 'positioning'. You have done your meticulous research, you can see what a professional enterprise should look like, and you have seen what a rubbish enterprise looks like. You have spoken to the customers and you can see which customers spend what and where.

For instance, you decide that you wish to do sales training and you see that medium enterprises are the ones using external trainers. The small firms don't appreciate the benefits and can't afford it anyway, while the large companies have their own in-house team. Therefore, your market is clearly defined and you must pitch in at a level of professionalism that will impress and reassure those people.

What traditionally happens is quite the reverse; instead of calculatingly tailoring their professionalism to their carefully selected market and persevering at this level, most enterprises permit their level of crapness to allow them to drift into doing business with the people who are prepared to put up with it.

MCPLUMBING

Imagine WalMart, McDonald's, Disney or Tesco deciding that a good new enterprise would be plumbing, tailoring and alterations, or gardening. What would that offer look like, do you think? The leaflet plops through your letterbox: 'McPlumbing for that leaking tap'. There would be a set of fixed prices, a 24-hour freefone number, a text number, a website. So let's ring them. "Thank you for ringing McPlumbing, I'm Judy, how can I help you? Certainly, when would it be convenient for one of our technicians to call? I have time slots between 9.00 to 11.00 am and 2.00 to 5.00 pm on your preferred day. Yes, between 2.00 and 5.00 pm will be fine.' At 2.30 pm a smart, uniformed polite person with the golden arch embroidered on his pocket arrives and puts on logoed slippers so as not to mark your carpet. The job is completed beautifully, neatly, and with no fuss or mess. The polite uniformed person asks you respectfully to sign a satisfaction form and when you have signed you are given a no-quibble two year guarantee. What do you do with the guarantee? You put it somewhere safe for at least two years. What other thing would you have kept for two years with the plumber's phone number on it?

Read the above paragraph again. Now tell me what impression that makes, and then tell me why you can't do everything that was done in this example. The clear leaflet, the beautifully answered phone, the reliable timing, the logoed uniform, the spotless and unobtrusive work, and finally the two year warranty. Which of those can't you do? There is nothing on that list that is cripplingly expensive – the smart uniform can be easily produced and with computer-controlled sewing machines, people can embroider your logo very cheaply indeed. The satisfaction form can be drawn up on your own computer and, don't panic, what will the two year guarantee actually cost you? If a dripping tap is fixed, in reality it doesn't drip again for many years so really you are on to a winner. The beautifully answered phone? Why would you do anything else? But, of course, almost every self-employed enterprise that you get in touch with falls down on every one of these checks – and notice, I have left out the leaflets because they are a whole huge issue themselves.

Think about this; if you have just read the above you may not be a plumber but I am willing to bet that you are an intelligent professional who has grasped and comprehended the implications of the McPlumbing story – and you can apply all of those professional aspects that you have understood to any enterprise you may be considering. In fact, if you get all of the professionalism into place as a result of your intellect, it might be easier to reverse the whole idea: use your inherent entrepreneurial skills and then learn to be a plumber, carpenter, bricklayer, dressmaker, cook, hairdresser – all enterprises that would benefit from a dose of professionalism. Consider for a moment the hugely successful franchises which offer basic skills like unblocking drains but seem to recruit very intelligent franchisees from all walks of life. Perhaps that is the secret of their success. When you apply intelligence and professionalism to a manual skill you can scoop the pot.

TRUST ME

So you need to be famous through reputation, but the greatest disaster you could achieve would be to become famous for being crap. I cannot emphasize this more toughly or more sincerely; the very heart and key to your success is to avoid at any cost any element of crapness or a reputation for crapness. Let me explain why.

Remember that the customer wants maximum benefit but minimum risk. New one-person enterprises could possibly offer good value – a benefit – but might be incompetent – a risk. May be unreliable – a risk. May be dishonest – a risk. You have just blown it on a score of three to one against. Just the tiniest whiff of shonkyness in the literature or the stationery will get the customer's risk juices flowing. The dirty, ill-maintained vehicle backs that up. A few minutes, or worse hours, or even worse, days late, just about seals the deal. All you then need is a complete dumbo answering the phone and you are done, dusted, and six foot under – complete with attractive headstone.

Whatever enterprises I have been using as examples, these rules can and should be applied to your planned enterprise before you start, and that pace should be maintained or improved forever. You should view your enterprise as a marathon and one that gets better as you go on. You start perfect and get better. So many people start by sprinting: "Yes, we can do that, we will work all night if we have to, we've kept to the budget by going to a bit of extra trouble, I've bound all the paper in a file to make it easier for you, of course we will do that . . . anything for a customer!" After a week of that they are completely knackered and go for option 'crap like all the rest'.

Look at the extremely rare, quivering, frightened creature that is our potential customer; when you see that poor thing cowering, what do you need to do to get its trust? Reassure and stroke – guarantees reassure, kept promises reassure, third party recommendations and testimonials reassure, appearance reassures, and the quality of communication reassures. Now apply these simple elements to your enterprise – if you can't tick all these boxes I cannot save you from your inevitable doom.

GIVE ME A RING

Phone answering and office services often get people into a sweat. This is the beginning of the reputation-building process – the beginning of the 'experience' of your enterprise. I have likened the successful self-employed person to the jungle guerrilla, travelling light with a bag of rice and an AK47. It's unlikely, you may think, for them to have a social secretary, but in these days of smart phones and portable media you, in theory, should always have a phone and the ability to respond to emails with you. Actually, at the time of writing this, revolutions are breaking out all over the world and Presidents are being toppled – not by Kalashnikovs but by iPhones.

Your mobile phone rings and as opposed to shrieking "YO!" or "Ello" or "Yep?" what prevents you from saying, "Gladys Spongs phone, how may we help you?"

Or, sometimes I'm told, "I get my Mum, wife, brother or dog to answer the phone." Picture that scene: "Hello?" "Is that International Food Hygiene? "No." "Not Mr Watson?" "Oh! You mean my Barry! He's on the bog at the moment, he had a curry last night . . . he could go through the eye of a needle!"

The solution is simply to train your mum. Insist, demand, bribe or threaten, the phone WILL be answered, "Thank you for calling International Food Hygiene, I'm Hilda, how may I help you?" "Oh yes, is Barry there, please?" "Who is calling, please?" "Terry Jenkins." "Well, Mr Jenkins, I'm afraid Mr Watson is in a meeting at the moment but if you could give me your number I will get him to ring you back in the next few minutes."

This is not a book on customer service but I do recommend that while doing your research you read a few of them (especially the ones I wrote!).

You may feel that I speak with forked tongue when I speak of travelling light, being a guerrilla, or paddling a kayak on the one hand, and then talking about prestigious full-out professionalism on the other, but there is no conflict – just don't have a kayak with holes in it.

INVEST IN QUALITY

The problem I find with new enterprises is that they tend to get their priorities wrong. They are prepared to lease hat stands, yet they shy away from investing in the customer-facing part of their enterprise that really can add value. Take yourself into any small shop right now and look at their price tickets – are they orange Day-Glo stars with badly handwritten prices on them? Who on earth invented and markets Day-Glo stars and what really, I ask you, was the thinking behind it? "I know, if we make these ghastly things, desperate small shopkeepers can make their depressing, failing shop look even more shonky and cheap!" And if it is your shop we are visiting, what were you thinking when you bought a packet of Day-Glo stars? It is unlikely to make you famous through good reputation but is likely to make you famous for being crap. That's positioning, OK?

I remember laughing at a cartoon of a little figure looking at a mountain-size pile of manure. At the top there was a sign which read, 'The Heap' and at the bottom a sign with an arrow which read 'You Are Here'. If that is where you want to be, that is where Day-Glo stars will put you, along with a whole host of other things like self-produced leaflets, horrid cheap business cards, a tatty personal appearance, an amateur website, dirty, rough-looking premises, or a tatty van that says 'You've tried the rest now try the best'.

It frustrates the living daylights out of me when small enterprises make these mistakes. This really isn't rocket science – if you watch what a large professional enterprise does and you offer the same standard of professionalism and appearance you cannot go wrong. Anything less than that is just rubbish and all you will do is earn a reputation of being 'not very good'. I chose those words carefully because words like 'outrageous', 'disgusting' and 'fearsome' are big, powerful, thought-provoking words which most enterprises also fail to achieve. They tend to go out with a whimper, not a bang, and are just not very good.

THE VIRTUAL MERCEDES

When I started my business coaching company I couldn't afford an office and couldn't afford a smart car, but my dilemma was that my competitors were the slickest of the slick and the sharpest of the sharp. Years ago, as I mentioned, I was involved in the scrap business. In the heart of big cities some of the people in the scrap game made considerable fortunes and probably had palatial homes in the country – the problem was that they were the sort of people who felt it was important to show that they were wealthy. Because of the difficulty of travelling in the city, it was unlikely that they could display their home lifestyle, therefore they would carry signs of wealth with them in the most portable form: the jewellery, the Cromby coat, gold fillings, and the Rolls Royce. For me, I couldn't let my clients see the office in my back bedroom, and it wasn't wealth I wanted to show signs of but professionalism: the good suit, silk tie, shiny shoes and crisp business cards. I couldn't afford the prestige car – in fact, I had a horrible old van which I had to park a few blocks away from my clients, but I could afford a prestige key ring which I could casually drop on the desk at a meeting, a sort of virtual Mercedes!

Let's just ruminate for a moment. Where are we with this? I want to stop here for a while and take stock before we move on. We have gone from the uniformed plumber to professionalism to my back bedroom, and the key messages from this are that:

- we need to be very clear about our market and who our customers are before working out what our positioning should be;

- from careful research we need to see and understand our competition in order to establish how our positioning compares;
- we have to test our offering against theirs and at least equal it in every detail, even if it means offering the same level of guarantee, money-back reassurance and the promise to put things right immediately. You may feel that this is a high cost option for a struggling, self-employed person, but if you lose your reputation it is going to cost you a lot more than that, it could cost you everything;

We have to understand that this is base camp – you cannot get away with being a bit more crap as long as it's a bit cheaper. Sure, if you want to open a truck stop café, it won't be bone china, Melba toast and roast quail, but it must at the very minimum be as good as any truck stop anywhere, or do you know what it is the trucks won't do . . . er . . . stop!

POINTS TO PONDER ON
'THE FAME GAME'

- Don't be afraid to put your own name to your enterprise.

- Get your name associated with the brilliance of what you do.

- Make sure your offer suits your intended market.

- Imagine the most professional organization you can think of, and simply do everything they do – you can't go wrong.

- Be famous . . . but never be famous for being bad.

- The faultless quality of your offer allays fears and promotes trust in your customers.

- Have the courage to guarantee what you do.

CHAPTER 13

ON THE SHOULDERS
OF GIANTS

. . . In which we consider the danger of pioneering and consider the benefits of slipstreaming behind the big boys.

THE WIND BENEATH MY WINGS

A nice little short cut you can take is to let someone else do some of the work. Large companies spend literally millions on product research, customer attitude surveys, and psychological marketing profiles – and because of that they tend to get things right . . . well, right by the time we get to see them, at any rate. So if you steal their ideas, you let them make the expensive mistakes.

If you feel nervous about stealing anything, don't worry yourself because our clever friends in marketing can gallop to our aid. No, it's not stealing any more, it's benchmarking or slipstreaming. These are slightly different. Benchmarking is about how your competitors – in our case, our huge competitors – set the standard. If you own a carnival, perhaps you could benchmark Disney – although it may be a dispiriting exercise, it would surely give you something to shoot for. The place is occupied by amusing, costumed characters that are recognizable from film and TV. Everyone is clean, cheery, knowledgeable and helpful. There is a wide choice of good, well-produced, wholesome food, and one single ticket lets you ride on everything as often as you like. That's part of the benchmark that Disney sets; how far are you away from that?

If you are in management training or something similar, does your large competitor send out reports in logoed binders, do they have a professional-looking newsletter, and what does their website look like? There is nothing there that cannot be achieved at modest cost and, indeed, without it, you are not in the game.

STAND BEHIND THE BIG KID

Slipstreaming is different. For many years I drove a weird little French car called a 2CV that, on the motorway in a headwind, virtually went backwards, it was so slow. The only way to make progress was to lock in dangerously close to a huge truck which would use its power to punch a hole in the air for me to drive through. So I and the truck made excellent forward progress – in fact, the car was so light that behind the biggest trucks I was virtually towed along unnoticed by the driver.

We can do the same thing with our enterprise. I have already rambled on about travelling light, kayaks, guerrillas, agility and so on. This means that we can lock in behind our big competitors and let them punch through the resistance without us even being noticed. Whilst enjoying edgy, innovative, rebel personalities, I can also see there is a risk with ground-breaking ideas.

When I was a kid, you would never see anything like olives, mangoes, real mayonnaise or ciabatta for sale – all now everyday items – but I bet the first person to sell any of these items had a financial disaster. In Europe, the burger business didn't exist until

McDonald's and Burger King punched their way through the resistance. It's only because of them that you could now open a burger bar in Luxemburg and expect to survive. If you had been the first burger bar in Europe you wouldn't have made it.

LIFE IN A GOLDFISH BOWL

What if you have got a new and innovative idea that isn't already being done so there is no big player's slipstream to fall in behind? Well, as I have said in previous chapters, new and innovative can be dangerous.

If you have discovered that there is no doubt whatsoever that it is more fun to watch TV with a goldfish bowl on your head, you will have an education job to do before others realize this too. OK, you have tried it on all your friends and there is no doubt, apart from the difficulty in breathing, that sitting in front of 'Star Trek' with a goldfish bowl on your head is better than sex. Tell me, a step at a time, where you go from there. Firstly, it is probably too late already, because your so-called friends who haven't died of asphyxiation have blurted out the idea on the social media, and before you have done anything to protect yourself the whole world is into the goldfish bowl thing. Therefore, we must keep our idea secret until we can protect it with the power of the law – another dangerous, futile and horribly expensive route to take.

A brilliant idea?
Some years ago, I had a colleague who had effectively put his life on hold and when asked why, he would touch his nose in a conspiratorial way and give his little speech: "Things will be different when my idea has made me rich." We would

always ask what it was and were met with, "Ah ha! Wouldn't you like to know!" To get the world patent and copyright protections for this thing ended up costing him his life savings and, if truth be known, a fair bit more. Finally, believing himself sufficiently protected and whilst receiving oaths of deepest secrecy from us (which I am just about to break), he led us to his shed where revelations and revealing would take place. He had spent hours and hours on this thing and it was fiendishly clever. Before I reveal all, it should be understood that he was a talented graphic designer – and there is an old cliché that warns that if the only tool you possess is a hammer then every problem will be seen as a nail. He designed lettering for companies which then had to be reproduced laboriously, expensively and, worst of all to him, inaccurately by sign writers. Lettering, to look good, has to be very carefully spaced so stencils and so on don't work. He had created a device that could allow the painter perfect accuracy and speed. Brilliant . . . and totally useless because, before he could market the clunky complicated thing, cheap computers learned how to laser cut vinyl letters. Game over! Savings gone.

My point is that, depressing though this may be, there really is no easy answer to this problem and if you want to be a successful self-employed person, innovative, dazzling and new ideas may not initially be the way to go. If you want a good income, pay your mortgage, have a few weeks holiday every year and a bit of cash to spend on wild living, then may I suggest that you model yourself on an enterprise that is already clearly successful. Mad inventors just seem to get madder and poorer!

RIP OFF

Going back to the goldfish bowl, there is an even worse fate waiting for us. The idea clearly works and is well protected; you launch with the twee name, 'Always Looking Through the Glass' or 'The World in a Goldfish Bowl' or something else equally cringe-making, and now you have to get it out there. The big companies have R&D departments. This used to stand for Research & Development: they would spend a fortune on hundreds of new ideas and products and one or two may break through to profit. A cynic now describes these R&D departments as 'Rip Off and Do the Same' departments! If you succeed and cannot saturate the market, they will circle you like sharks looking for an opening. What have you protected? The goldfish bowl – but maybe it is the lack of oxygen that enhances the experience, therefore a bucket with eye-holes may work. Once you get the international corporations after you, trouble will follow. I am not saying that innovation is a bad thing, but it's cheaper and more profitable if you apply your innovative juices to established ideas that just need to be made better with your talents.

Or, you could completely turn the tables and 'Rip Off and Do the Same' yourself. I am now on dangerous ground myself because I may be inciting you to an illegal act, so therefore the following has to be seen as a philosophical discussion to be entitled 'Your luck and how far can you push it'.

Old Mcdonald
McDonald's protect their brand ferociously. I believe that there was a restaurant owned by a Mr Macdonald that was, believe it or not, called 'Macdonald's'. McDonald's (they of the golden arches) took exception to even that. The reason for their toughness is the value of their brand, but also, strangely enough, the vulnerability of it McDonald's will sell you a McDonald's franchise for many thousands of pounds, but if you just want to open a burger bar it costs a fraction of that. Why pay all that money to McDonald's? Because

the name and the specific quality and consistency of the product guarantees customers and, therefore, a good income.

I live in a medium sized town that has two McDonald's – one in the town centre and the other a drive-through on the northern fringes. When I want a Big Mac, I have at least a fifteen minute journey each way, guaranteeing cold food. Answer: my part of town could support another McDonald's. Then the simple solution is to open one. What you can't afford to pay is the thousands in franchise fees and profit share. Then don't! Just build a burger bar, call it McDonald's, have the same menu, the same prices, the same uniforms, same opening hours, the same quality, and the same logo and colours. Within about thirty seconds of opening, McDonald's lawyers will have shut you down, but for what? What could you get away with before they could get you?

Close to the wind

Let's examine supermarket own brands – boy, do they sail close to the wind. By the way, that's a nice expression, 'close to the wind'. When a sailboat is full out with every rope tight, the wind howling in the rigging and the crew driven to work perfectly by the fear of failure and a watery grave, at one moment the boat, in sheets of white spray, is at its fastest, the next (if the rudder is pushed the wrong way) it is at its upside down-est. You can run your enterprise like that, exciting, fast and rewarding, but that way is a little too nerve wracking for me.

Anyway, back to own brands: what the supermarkets have realized is that they can make far more money from their own brands than the global brand products. They also realized that the global brands have become instantly recognizable by shape, colour and size, without the customer needing to actually read the label. Take Kellogg's Cornflakes. If Cheapo Supermarkets Inc wants to get the best price for their own cheapo cornflakes, then give the pack red lettering and a big green and red chicken on it. Of course, Kellogg's hate this and take legal action – the crime is called 'Trading Off'.

OK, not a chicken, but maybe a green and red guinea fowl? Too close? Maybe a pattern of green and red shapes that could be arranged into a chicken. Take yourself to a supermarket and see how close they get – they are getting away with it and they consider it is worthwhile. I am not suggesting that you open up with your copy McDonald's and wait to get sued, but surely you could work out, with a bit of research, what you could get away with. Perhaps two friends, Donald and Mack, could open a Mack and Donald's. Perhaps you could have a golden W standing for World of Burgers, but that's not the point. The reason I have picked on poor old McDonald's is because it is a brilliant, successful and highly profitable company, and they spend a huge amount of their colossal wealth and power staying that way. You could never have access to those sorts of resources and you should trust that, on the whole, McDonald's are completely right; therefore if you do exactly what they do (within the law), you can't go wrong.

Has a McDonald's ever gone bust or lost money? I should think that, on the whole, it is unlikely. Look at the menu: Big Mac, Quarter Pounder, chicken sandwich, fillet of fish, two sizes of fries, thick shakes and volcanically hot apple pies. To the uninitiated, the temptation before the appearance of the knobbly stick would be to say, "What this place needs is turkey burgers." Oh really? I bet McDonald's, at great expense, have already tried them and binned them. Legend has it that if McDonald's try a certain product and it doesn't make a prescribed level of profit, they bin it immediately. The truth is that at great expense they have done it right. Don't change a thing: the menu, the opening hours, the prices, the uniform, the cleanliness, and the little speech at the till, "Would you like the meal deal? Go large with the fries?" The point is that you can let someone bigger and stronger than you do the dangerous work of punching a hole in the headwind.

An interesting exercise for you is to have a look at the small independent fast-food outlets that are not McDonald's or any of the other prestige fast-food chains. Why do they look rubbish? No, really, this is useful, go with a pad and pen and write down every-thing they are doing wrong, why they are not McDonald's, and why they will go bust. I bet you can see every detail – the grubbi-ness, the surly staff, the poor position, the nasty food – so here is a thing, you can see it all, but the owner can't. Will this blindness affect your enterprise?

SETTING THE STANDARDS

Of course, I am not suggesting that you all rush out and open a burger bar, but this slipstreaming/benchmarking can be applied to any enterprise. Want to start a bed and breakfast? Have a look at Holiday Inn Express: plain, clean rooms, no ornaments, no smell of cabbage. OK, you may say you hate that, it's not homely or welcoming, like you. Well, they spend millions getting it right – they get it right and they make money. You may have better, more profit-able, ideas but it is like climbing Everest with experienced guides and Sherpas and saying, "I know a better way", then untying the rope and setting off. Well, you may be right but you are SO on your own. You bet your house, your money, your future prosperity and your life.

Whatever enterprise you have chosen (unless you are a pioneer), there will be another enterprise somewhere that is at the top of that particular tree. You may have ideas of your own and want to work differently, but bear in mind that someone else has done a lot of hard work to get where they are and it would be foolish not to benefit from it and take what you can from looking at how they do it.

FRANCHISING

An example of how this works commercially is franchising. Someone else does all the hard work of establishing a business and then you pay them to, in effect, rent that idea.

I work with franchise organizations on their customer development strategies for franchisees. Therefore, so as not to risk annoying any of them, for this exercise we will invent an unlikely franchise – let's say a tree pruning service called 'Mr Tree'. There is a nice little cartoon figure who is winking and holding a sparkling pair of shears, it is a well established franchise with profitable members all over the country. There are only three areas left and the price for one is £50,000. If you do exactly what you are told (which you have to) you will make £50,000 a year. You also have to pay a percentage of your takings on top of the initial fee. The biggest problem I get is with franchisees whinging about the cost and how they feel some of the publicity material and vehicle liveries are unnecessary. Well, they are necessary! Again, the franchise operations with their uniforms, smart vehicles, clear menu prices, guarantees and professional leaflets and stationary have got it right.

What am I saying here? What I am suggesting is that people resist spending money on the things that give a feeling of professionalism and competence because they feel that it is not relevant to the core business. The problem is that the core business is less relevant than we think.

POINTS TO PONDER ON
'ON THE SHOULDERS OF GIANTS'

- Big companies spend a fortune on getting it right so let them do the hard work of breaking new ground.

- Big companies set the standard that customers expect. Try not to offer anything less.

- Self-employed people fail because they get things wrong. In my opinion, McDonald's don't get anything wrong, therefore do exactly what they do and you won't go wrong.

- It is possible that, as self-employed people, we simply cannot afford to innovate.

- If we have a great idea, a lot of people will work very hard to steal it.

- Let other people test the good ideas while you make the money.

CHAPTER **14**

THE PROFESSIONAL APPROACH

. . . In which we see the benefits of a professional approach, and we dissect our enterprise and use the example of Fred to find which bits work and which don't.

A PROPER HAIRDRESSER

Years ago, on one of my courses – a self-employment seminar – I had a woman who was a truly fabulous hairdresser who had worked in the capital's top salons. For various reasons, she had found herself without a job and also without much money. The solution was to take the tools (scissors and a hairdryer) and go round to peoples' homes where she did a great job. What great job is that, then? "Why," I hear you reply, "doing peoples' hair, of course." Ah, but here's the rub. One day, one of her customers said, "Don't come next month, come the month after." When she did go back it looked like the woman's head had been set on fire!

"What happened?" the hairdresser asked. "Oh, it was my boy's wedding and I thought I should go to a proper hairdresser." A proper hairdresser! Reflect on that statement for a moment. If you do accountancy from home, will clients be tempted to go to a 'proper accountant' rather than you?

A LITTLE TREASURE

Despite your skill or diligence or ability to do the job, an enterprise must take into account the surrounding things that do not apparently relate specifically to the core skill. Rich people are usually rich because they are often very shrewd, and I find they indulge in a secret practice of developing 'little treasures'. Being rich and clever, unlike the majority of the public, they do value core skills and realize that their prey, who are incompetent at professionalism but are brilliant at the core skill, can be had on the cheap and will become little treasures. "I have a man who does my gardening, he's a bit smelly but he is a little treasure. I can't remember the last time we paid him!" "She is a bit odd but she does all my dressmaking by hand, we pay her pennies, she is a little treasure." Do you want to be a 'little treasure'? No? Then shape up!

Paid on appearance

OK, you don't want, or can't afford, to pay franchise fees, but you can't let your standards of presentation fall below what they offer; tattiness costs money. What could the hairdresser have done?

Take two women who do beauty treatments from home. The first one you visit meets you at the door with a smile. She is in a pair of comfy jeans and slaps a big mug of coffee in your hands.

She leads the way up the stairs to her back bedroom, booting the kids' toys out of the way. The cat is slung off the bed before you lie on it for your facial. Actually, apart from a few flea bites, she does a great job and could become your 'little treasure' but . . . the other woman meets you at the front door in a white, mandarin-collared medical coat with, and get this, a gold name badge. She is the only one there and you know her name. She carries a big black appointment book in which your name, time and agreed treatments have been written. You are led to the back bedroom, only it's not a back bedroom, it's a proper consulting room with a treatment couch, venetian blinds, spot lights, shelves displaying complementary products and potions, and leaflet dispensers with professional leaflets and price lists of the various options. FACT – she will make more money than the other woman.

Invest in your image

The whole point of being self-employed is that you can kick back, chill out and make good money without, in some cases, even setting foot outside your front door, but that does not mean you can afford to be rubbish. When people spend on a car, a computer and a hat stand, they somehow feel that it's not so important to invest in the image of their enterprise – which brings us neatly to the subject of leaflets, catalogues and other publicity. Leaflets are a weird thing and you may not even need them, but if you feel that you do, they had better be good or you will advertise that you are crap and a bit of an amateur.

Good design is very expensive and when you spend a few thousand on your logo, image and publicity material when you haven't even got a car, it hurts. What I used to do is to offer a good prize like a mountain bike or a TV to design students – I would get thirty or so good designs and use the winner for the price of a mountain bike. Whatever you do, don't let the computer do it – it stands out like the balls on a dog and just shouts 'back bedroom', 'wet behind the ears', 'amateur halfwit'.

Again, pause for thought: the cheap paper, home-printed flyer drops through the door with the inevitable little clip-art figure clutching a megaphone and shouting, "You've tried the rest now try the best!" Does that float your boat? Does it get your juices flowing. Do you rush to the phone to do business with them? No, of course not, so don't even think of doing it yourself, it just makes you look like a loser.

THE IMAGINARY FRANCHISE

Whatever enterprise you choose, a great exercise for testing it is to imagine that you will turn it into a franchise. It doesn't matter what enterprise you have chosen, any one could be a franchise, from accountancy to business skills training, to house painting, or even party food. So let's pick party food as an example.

You have been told by your friends that your vol-au-vents are to die for, your nibbles take them to another place, and your small jellies provoke a rapture of pure delight. "You should cater for parties," they tell you. OK, you have ignored the warning about twee names and you start 'Party Time', the fun food company for any party. Small adverts, leaflets, cards in shop windows, the website and word of mouth lead you to a reasonable amount of work. In a way, businesses like this one are the most disappointing for me because they do well for a bit and then they just sort of peter out. They are like spring flowers which pop up all colours, perfumes and busy bees, only to disappear a few days later because they fail to have deep roots. But while the enterprise survives, people suggest that they would like to open a 'Party Time' in their town.

A kit of parts
Now here's the thing to think about; how do you put 'Party Time' into a reproducible package, a replicable kit of parts? I am not asking you to do this because you are likely to franchise your

business, but because it will help you to focus, professionalize and become established.

The potential franchisee will ask how much it costs to set up, how much they can expect to make, where they will find the business, and how hard it is to master the skills required. Well, can you answer those questions about your enterprise?

Let's have a look at the 'Party Time' franchise. How will the food be distributed to the parties – currently it's put in the back of the odd car or taxi. OK, it gets a bit battered and warm on hot days but would you invest in a special vehicle? Maybe a small chilled van painted in the franchise's pink candy stripe and logo . . . well, it's not my business so don't look at me.

The question is: what would you advise your franchisee to do? Vehicles like that don't come cheap. Where do they find the work? Oh yes, that's right, leaflets, small adverts, cards in shops, the website and word of mouth – which one works the best? Out of the small ads, which designs brought the most responses, which are the best publications to go in, how well does the website score, which part of it elicits the best response? The cards in the shops are, of course, professionally designed so they, and not just ghastly scrappy bits of paper, can be handed out in packs to the franchisee. You will have formalized the word of mouth thing, won't you, by giving out bundles of recommendation cards that earn discounts or prizes for recommendation. Don't worry, you won't have to remember all that, because you are going to put it into a precise and easy-to-read manual.

How would you like the franchisees to look? Nice, smart, pink candy stripe jackets, jaunty paper hats, proper food handling gloves, no jewellery, and all clean and fragrant. The food should be consistently prepared to the laminated recipe card and presented on special trays, linen with logoed napkins with all the correct garnishes – just like you do now and every other time with no slip or reduction in quality.

Even things like suppliers should be consistent. Can you see that by analyzing and formalizing your enterprise in this way, it gives you the opportunity to analyze it in a detached objective manner?

Remember those tatty fast food outlets – you could see trouble brewing but the owners couldn't. There is a very, very old business joke that says, "When you are up to your arse in alligators, it is very hard to remember that you set out to drain a swamp." Just climb up on the bank once in a while to count your alligators and to see where the sluice gate is.

FRED'S GARAGE

Now you have dealt with all this, let me explain the problem of Fred's Garage and ask you to help me with it. As an adviser to small enterprises, this and similar situations are constant problems that I come across and are hard to solve. The thing with the main authorized dealers of cars is that they have a workshop full of engineers, and the work as it comes is distributed to the engineers by relating difficulty to skill. You buy your shiny new car and a few months into ownership it is in either for its first service or to tidy up a few niggles. This thing is your pride and joy so, of course, you take it to the main dealer in order for the correct people to set to work on your treasured vehicle. Routine service – who do you think that is given to? Of course, the least experienced person there, probably the apprentice.

These garages often have someone called Fred. Fred is a brilliant intuitive engineer who knows, through experience, every aspect of your particular vehicle – he may even be the shop foreman. The hourly rate charged by garages is eye-watering, say, £120 per hour plus a big juicy mark-up on any spare parts used. It stands to reason that if the apprentice does the job at £10 per hour, a lot more money can be made than if Fred does it for £20 per hour. The only little drawback is that the apprentice is a clumsy, inexperienced gibbon, so anything complex or difficult should be given to Fred. There is also another matter to consider: when you tell them your brakes or whatever need fixing, they can quote a price for the job. How do they know how long the job is going to take? Do you think it is experience? No, it isn't. They use a book that sets down the hours for each job. The book is generous in its estimates (generous to the garage, not you) and that is what you will be charged. This is how it works in the garage's favour. Say your car needs a clutch; the book says six hours labour. Someone like Fred could do that in three. You pay £720 for three hours work; Fred gets £60. The Freds of this world kick up at this so they are paid a modest bonus for speed – sometimes even their hourly rate. For example, the book says six hours, Fred earns £120 for three hours work. The apprentice shouldn't even be allowed near jobs like that but on simple routine jobs the gap narrows and so does the profit. On oil changes, it's half an hour; that is how long it takes, no matter who does it.

Pastures new

The Freds of this world eventually tire of this and look for pastures new. To them the arithmetic is simple: if they open their own garage and charge even half price, they would be ahead of the game. A clutch would cost £360 – a bargain for you and a bonus for Fred. Despite the exorbitant charges, main dealers go bust with monotonous regularity so we have to understand why that happens. The answer is overheads. The new cars you see in their huge glittering showrooms have to be bought on borrowed money and there is that huge glittering showroom itself – loads of staff, managers and salespeople all conspire to cost a fortune. Fred, therefore, when opening his enterprise, must avoid these overheads, so when choosing premises he must be careful. A great area is found underneath some railway arches, loads of room for a modest rent. There we have it, 'Fred's Garage', not even a twee name, a perfect enterprise; you can take your pride and joy to this place and the best engineer in the whole world for your model of car will work on it with obsessive diligence for half the price, without the gibbon of an apprentice being allowed anywhere near it – even for routine jobs. It's like having a world-famous brain surgeon syringing your ears . . . and yet you are still not tempted to use the services of Fred. A few clever people realize that Fred is a 'little treasure' but the rest of us are frightened to do it.

In Fred's shoes

As I have already said, this is a thinking exercise. Using your intelligence, and perhaps some of the ideas in this book, put yourself in Fred's position and plan the launch and establishment of Fred's Garage. Remember, like the rest of us, Fred is a one-person start-up and funds are limited. He possesses a beautiful professional tool kit but he must invest in the special tools and computer that every modern car needs before he can fix it. You are in a weird position here because for this exercise you are playing the part of Fred, but you are really one of Fred's potential customers. Setting aside all the warranty issues – in fact, let's imagine your car is just out of warranty – why won't you take it to Fred? Picture the premises in your mind and tell me what's putting you off. Is there anything about Fred's demeanor or attitude that is a deal breaker?

While you think how you would change Fred and his garage, let's consider the big thing that's holding you back from doing business with him. It is fear. It is the risk you take. Tell me, what risk is that? You see this backstreet garage and you feel that you would be taking a risk by leaving your car there. Write a list of those risks is he going to treat your car with respect; will he be driving about in it; is the place secure and insured; and most of all, is he competent? But hang on a minute, the whole point and pivot of this tale hangs on the fact that Fred is super competent. What did you say? Oh, Fred didn't tell you that! Most small backstreet repair shops have a story. If you speak to that oily guy with the cigarette dangling out of his mouth, you will get a life history that speaks of long apprenticeships, college certificates and race mechanics. True, there are chancers who have no qualifications at all and may well wreck your car or even steal it, but we're working with Fred and we know that he is good, so how do we communicate that to the customers?

Prestige presentation

While you consider that, have a think about how you will communicate your professionalism to your customers.

For some reasons that are too tiresome to explain, I found myself
driving a prestige German car for a while and my experience of the
dealership is worth recounting. When I arrived, a smiling receptionist who was expecting me took my keys and tagged them with a
big bold tag with the garage's logo on one side and all my details
on the other. They also took all my contact details and neatly wrote
them down. They told me when they expected to have the car ready
but always pleased me by ringing much earlier than predicted
and telling me it was ready ahead of schedule. Through a special
window I could see the workshop, which had a polished tiled floor
so clean that you would gladly eat your dinner off it. The engineers
wore spotless overalls in the company's colours, all with the logo
embroidered on the pocket and the engineer's name also embroidered on (badges scratch paintwork). When I came to collect the
car, a custom dust cover was removed with a flourish from the seat
and hanging from the mirror was a card with the engineer's name,
picture and his comments about the work. The bill was presented
in a small folder with a list of services and special offers – and
another thing was that, whatever the quote for the job had been,
the bill would always be just a little bit less (a nice touch). The
reception was immaculate, there was coffee, a tidy waiting area,
and a large neat board with the cost of the fixed price services on
it. A prestige dealership for prestige cars.

Do the same

There is nothing here that Fred cannot do at modest cost (except
that he will have to play the part of receptionist as well). On the
other hand, he must lose the grubby overall, the bills written out
on the backs of envelopes, the 'no idea when it will be ready' attitude, the piles of old tyres kicking around the place, the cigarettes
and empty oil cans. Fred would argue that this is all flim flam and
his skill is all that matters. Well, my answer to that is, "Fred, give

me that old flim flam, but then back it up with information, assurances, and guarantees."

To return to the start of this exercise, one of the puzzles that it poses is that Fred is a brilliant and highly qualified technician, and probably, in your own field, so are you. The problem is that the potential customer doesn't know this.

POINTS TO PONDER ON
'THE PROFESSIONAL APPROACH'

- When your friends and customers look at you, do they think you are a proper enterprise, or are you somebody's little treasure?

- It is up to you how you look, but be sure that it is a luxury you can afford.

- Good design and presentation may be expensive but it can be money well spent.

- It can be helpful to imagine that you are selling your business idea as a franchise to another person. Write an instruction booklet with all the things that work and all the things that don't work. This is a great way to analyze your business.

- You might be brilliant, but don't forget to show and tell your customers that you are.

- Find a way to positively communicate the good things that you will do for your customers. It is no good just doing them, you have to tell your customers that you are doing them.

- Our biggest hurdle is removing the risk that our customers feel they are taking by doing business with us.

CHAPTER 15

REASSURANCE

. . . In which we learn to tell our story and reassure our customers big and small.

GOAT POLITICS

One of the keys for the well-qualified self-employed is to tell a good, well-presented and believable story – remember, maximum benefit with minimum risk. A good story can remove a load of those risks from the customer's mind and in some cases it can generate a premium. Just think, what bothers you about buying fast food: poor quality ingredients, animal welfare, poor preparation, and stuff frozen and microwaved? Do you have a fast food joint that avoids all of these things? That is nice, but it won't make any difference to the customer if they don't know that and you haven't told them your story – unless, of course, you are a customer of the British sandwich chain, Pret A Manger. Here, you will receive a sandwich packed in a rustic, environmentally-sound cardboard wrapper which, more to the point, carries the 'story', something like, 'This sandwich was prepared in the last thirty minutes by our chefs, with golden free range organic eggs and salad washed in spring water. The bread is from stone-ground Norfolk wheat grown by Farmer Watkins.' I just made all that up, but if you go there you will find I'm not far off.

Years ago, on one of my courses I had a lady who kept goats and sold the cheeses. The cheeses sold for around £1 each and she could sell all she could make (the restaurants found her to be a little treasure). The problem was that her capacity was a couple of hundred cheeses a week. "Why don't you buy in goats' milk from other farms?" I suggested. She looked at me in a very weird way and replied enigmatically, "Aha, now you're getting into goat politics!" From that I assumed that output could not be increased, so what we did was to wrap and box the cheese in a nice country-style (but cheap) wooden box lined with wood shavings, but the key was a small booklet attached to the cheese by a golden thread. In it was written the story of Ivy Farm Cotswold goats' cheese: 'Goats that have roamed these hills for nine centuries, a rare animal that is fond of eating the windfall pears and rare herbs that grow from the craggy Cotswold stone. People often declare that in this delicate and subtle flavoured cheese, there is definitely an herby note of pear sweetness . . . Judy Truneon is the twelfth generation of goat farmers who lovingly fashion these sought-after local cheeses . . .'. You get the idea, I'm sure. We took them round the tourist areas and allowed restaurants to reproduce the words from the booklet. The cheeses are bought as gifts at well over £5 each (and she still can't make enough!)

Returning to Fred

Our friend Fred from the previous chapter has got to find a way of doing the same. A website, of course, helps with that – but more of websites later. He could put a nicely produced board on the wall with a bit of life history, perhaps some pictures of Fred when he was a race mechanic working on the world champion's car. He could put a short résumé in his leaflets and in the little paste-board folder where he puts the bill. The point is that all of this offers reassurance; so does a money-back guarantee, warranted work, loads and loads of testimonials, and a professional appearance.

WHAT'S YOUR STORY?

An exercise that you could try is to take a piece of paper and write down your 'story' in a way that it could be presented to your customer to reassure them that you are competent to do the job that they would like you to do. For example, in a street near me a new shoe shop opened, clearly owned by a single individual. I feel that her business would take an enormous step forward if, in the window, she had presented her story, i.e. 'Doris Perkins has worked for twenty years and been trained in the highly specialist area of childrens feet'. . . and so on. Therefore, any parent walking past would feel reassured and obliged to use this 'professional' to correctly handle their childrens' feet in preference to one of the high street chains.

KNOW YOUR CUSTOMER

Just think for a moment about your enterprise or planned enterprise. Consider the risk your customers will be taking by coming with you and how you can provide evidence that will reassure them. For instance, I know a sales trainer who says if sales don't increase by at least ten percent you don't have to pay for the training – now that's reassuring!

This chapter is about how we can use tools, such as our story, our appearance, our professionalism and our guarantees, to reassure our customers. The problem for the self-employed individual is that they won't necessarily just be doing business with individuals – in fact, a lot of self-employed opportunities come from doing business in the corporate world where all of the usual customer problems occur but are multiplied a thousandfold. As we have discussed, one of the things every customer likes to avoid is risk, but again this is multiplied when it comes to dealing with corporate customers and the self-employed person has to be acutely aware of this and possibly might have to consider whether the corporate route is one they want to take. A danger for us self-employed people is that a corporate customer can provide us with so much work there is no room for any other customers, so if we do screw up we could lose everything. Having said all that, there is a way of gaining the confidence of the corporate customer, but just be aware of the pitfalls if you are considering a service to corporate buyers. Fred may convince us, but could he go to 'Consolidated Megabuck Inc' and get their fleet servicing contract? I doubt it and you know I think I might counsel him not to try.

I think at this juncture, a key point has been raised for us aspiring self-employed, and that is . . . know your customer. If you remember, we discussed how the marketing department of huge corporations is obsessed with the concept of positioning. When I worked in advertising many many years ago, we (I am sure politically incorrectly) classified people into class types, something like A1, A, B, B2, C, C2 and so on. A-type people bought Rolex watches and drove Aston Martins; C-type people ate burgers and went on cheap rowdy package holidays. Of course, it is all a bit more complex than that, because a C-type who comes into money thinks that wearing a gold Rolex gives him a badge that says, 'I am an A', and all the As start wearing beaten-up Swatch watches so as not to appear 'flash and over-eager'. For example, in positioning you would think Coke would go for the trendy rock-kids having fun thing, which on the whole they do, but hold on up there a moment. Coke has been around for years and was hugely popular in the '50s and '60s. Maybe a Harley thunders across a desert in a cloud of dust and thumping rock music, there is a muscular rider and a slim shapely woman, their faces hidden by dark visors. When they pull into the deserted diner and crack open two ice-cold Cokes, we see that they are 'Best Agers' (no, really, that is what marketers call old people). The first geriatric Coke advertisement! Would it work? Would they do it? Be assured that, if they did, they would have a very well-thought-out reason. They would be positioning or re-positioning Coke. This is because they know their customers.

The self-employed have a frightening tendency to put out the proposition that appeals to themselves and hope that some customers might coincide with it. This is because they don't know their customers and, in fact, have no idea who their customers could possibly be. When planning your enterprise, do you have an absolutely clear idea who your customers are likely to be? There is no point in impressing, attracting and reassuring, people who have no intention or ability of doing business with you.

One-legged Scotsmen

We self-employed may feel we know our customers, but it is an unconscious knowing. We rarely sit back and categorize our customers and analyze where our work is coming from. But if we did, this should give us two options: one is to realize that we have a unique appeal to, maybe, one-legged Scotsmen and we look through every medical record to find amputees with a Mac or Mc in front of their surnames; or, secondly, we can realize that by making only competitively priced left shoes we are restricting our market and we should change to broaden our appeal.

In the case of Fred's Garage, he might well be advised to put away thoughts of the corporate work and concentrate on his core business. If I were him, I wouldn't go for the bottom of the market either. I would imagine that the three or more year-old cars owned by a mature owner who needs looking after would be a rich vein for Fred. Also, although it may be seen as a risky strategy, Fred could be niche. If he is Ford – or more to the point – BMW-trained, he could offer himself as an independent specialist, but he can't step those customers down too far from what they are used to, things like the BMW logo, a dish of sweeties and a clean waiting area.

DO YOUR HOMEWORK

The above are all assumptions to make the point in this book. For you, it will mean meticulous research; perhaps a written description of your customer and some written and photographic examples of their current experience. Is this too much work if you just want to paint people's houses, fix their jeans, or open a burger trailer? Look, your future prosperity, well-being and sanity depend on you getting this right, so do your homework. If you can't be arsed, then that's OK, but you probably won't be arsed to flip burgers for the next twenty years either – so there's your answer.

THE BIGGER THE BUSINESS, THE BIGGER THE RISK

The problem is that some of us come from a corporate environment and see that management training, corporate restructuring, event organizing, and so on, are where we need to be. It is possible to do business with corporations; I have a friend who is a one-person corporate catering genius who has sold her talent to a number of huge corporations where she organizes and manages all of the staff dining – but, boy oh boy, is she sharp and professional. So, it can be done, but the risk challenge is multiplied a million times and we cannot afford to slip up.

Big decisions

To put this into context, let me explain. One of my occupations is to write books that analyze and explain the selling and buying process. Writers of the old-fashioned sales training books used to obsess about meeting what was referred to as the 'decision maker'. This would lead to the mistake of imagining that you would move up the food chain for greater success. This assumed that, if you could get in to see the CEO and convince them, the job would be yours, but CEOs tend to feel that they are above all that and would certainly kick decisions about window cleaning, food or training down to their minions! I won't bore you with all the details, but if you are really interested you could read one of my sales books, try *Irresistible Persuasion* or *Resistance is Useless*, or, for a more light-hearted approach, *The Way of the Dog*! The area I want to just touch on now, though, is big decisions. Just because we are a small enterprise does not mean that the decision to use us is a small one.

There is a rule-of-thumb measure to discover if the thing is a big decision. Let's just examine what isn't a big decision. A child has a few pence, child wants a candy bar, the bar costs a few pence, child decides to buy candy bar, job done.

The measure for big decisions is: (1) it takes time to conclude the sale successfully; (2) it is unlikely an immediate purchase will be made; (3) more than one sales visit is required; (4) often, more than one person is involved in the buying decision: (5) and for us this is the biggy . . . the buyer is cautious because a buying mistake would have major repercussions.

A troubled past

A little bit of a history lesson here. In the late 20th century, IBM was the absolute king of the computer and business machine market. Their executives dressed so smartly and sharply that they set the trend for every international business person who wanted or needed to look the part. The whole image thing – their pro-fessionalism and on-the-ball attitude – earned them the revered nickname 'Big Blue'. The point of me telling you all this is that there was a very telling saying that went, 'You don't get fired if you buy Big Blue', which would suggest that one may well get fired if one bought from someone less well known or risky; in other words, if they bought from you! However, by being such a leviathan, IBM became too slow to change and innovate at the correct pace and have declined from those earlier glory days. But even at their height, not every solution they offered was perfect for the customer, but still people would work with them – sometimes disappointingly – because of the words, "you don't get fired if you buy Big Blue" ringing in their ears.

Frustration

When I started my business-to-business training all those years ago, I would get so frustrated when I met the sales managers or HR people. I knew I could do a great job for them, I was sure I had them convinced with my presentation, and then I would get that phone call – or worse – letter, "We are grateful for your time and were impressed with your presentation but for this financial year we have decided to remain with our current supplier." "But you told me they were rubbish!" "Yes, they are rubbish, but better the devil you know and all that." It used to drive me wild but then I realized that the minions that I needed to do business with literally feared for their jobs; they were safe if their decision was no decision. What I was failing to do was to tell them a convincing story, one that reassured and convinced them that I was safe to do business with.

What are you offering the large corporates: business intelligence, recruitment, product design, subatomic nanotechnology, or even window cleaning?

OK, let's take the window cleaning. Megacorp have had their windows cleaned for forty years by Bloggs & Company. Their standards have declined while their prices have risen. Surely this is an opportunity for a bright spark like you? So you find your decision maker . . . well it won't be the El Supremo, he will have delegated stuff like cleaning and maintenance to someone like the Facilities Manager, who in this case we will call Mr Perkins.

Sell, sell, sell

Could we just stop at this point, because my 'thing' is sales. In my heart, I am a persuader and a situation like this would normally get me to write a few thousand words on how this guy would be persuaded; how to crush all resistance to the requests for an appointment; how to evaporate any objections; how to make him chuckle with glee at our prices; and how to make him sign on the dotted line while dribbling with anticipatory excitement. But this is not the place for that detail here. To be fair, in preparation for this adventure you must have some selling skills under your belt, and there are some great books, DVDs, websites and seminars (and not all presented by me) that will help. My only tip, then, before we move on, is that when in the presence of a customer or potential customer, i.e. everybody, we should develop the habit of having an intention to sell.

Back to Mr Perkins. Using the above-mentioned wiles we get to see him, we convince him and start the window cleaning on Monday. His mightiness is wandering around his domain with his entourage of lickspittles and notices something different. His first reaction, whether or not what he sees is good or bad, is, "Perkins! Perkins, where are you, man? Perkins, get here!" "Yes, your great worshipfulness, how may we be of humble service?" "What's this? "New window cleaners, light of my life." "New window cleaners? What's wrong with Bloggs? My father hired Bloggs."

Perkins in trouble

This is the sort of conversation Perkins wanted to avoid and now he has to, second-hand, justify your presence. While you may not feel that window cleaning is a big decision, for Perkins it sure is because it so fits that criteria, "The buyer is cautious because a buying mistake would have major repercussions." The buyer in this case, Perkins, could lose his job or at least be in terrible disgrace. And if he does nothing? "Perkins?" "Yes, your highness?" "Windows are looking a bit grubby." "It's Bloggs, sir, they are letting things slip." "Mmm, I'll get on to it – I'm playing golf with

Bloggs Senior. I'll have a word." It doesn't matter whether he does or he doesn't, Perkins is off the hook.

As a small newcomer to this market, we must be aware that whoever chooses to use us against the 'safe' (if crap) alternative is taking a massive gamble.

Outstanding and remarkable

First, then, we must be better than good, more than professional; we must be OUTSTANDING and REMARKABLE. That means so wonderfully, awesomely good that we get noticed for the wonderfulness of what we provide and, when we do, pass the credit on to the Mr Perkins of this world. "I am Sir John Timbersaw and I would just like to congratulate you on the food at our staff party." "Well, if it wasn't for the wonderful briefing and help that Mr Perkins gave us, we would never have been able to do it."

Secondly, understand that, by being brilliant, you have the potential to create enemies. By virtue of what you do you are going there to make their business better and more efficient. Not everybody will welcome that – they may have to work faster because of your efficient redesign, or they may have been receiving juicy little backhanders. If you don't get in there and sort this out, you will find the honeymoon over very quickly.

STABBED IN THE BACK

When I was in the scrap game, we won a contract where the boss's obsession was having enough bins, sacks and containers. I was aware of that and flooded the job with all the sacks and containers they needed, yet they still rang and rang, complaining they were short of sacks until we lost the job. It turns out that an employee was a relative of the old, inefficient contractor and was just stealing and vandalizing everything as fast as we could deliver it.

The solution is to return to the apocryphal decision-maker thing. What we have to realize is that, in a corporate environment, there are a lot of people involved in any decision. If we build a faster, more efficient machine we may get to see the CEO, we may convince him with our tales of increased production, but we must also make a strong financial case to the finance director, a great mechanical case to the works engineer, and finally a tale of increased bonus to the poor sap on the factory floor who has got to work twice as hard. In other words, in a corporate environment we may have many different customers, and each one will have to have a story that reassures them, a custom-made story that suits their particular situation. It cannot be a case of one size fits all. Know your customer and tailor your proposition to reassure them.

Next, we must allay the fears and risks by offering get-outs, guarantees and reassurances. They say the best way to eat an elephant is one piece at a time "Perkins!" "Yes, your mightiness?" "What's going on here?" "Well, sir, some new people have offered a money-back guarantee on improved, more cost effective, window cleaning. They are just doing the ones in the small annex for now as a sort of trial. If nothing else, it will keep Bloggs on their toes!" "Carry on, Perkins!"

The whole point of all this is that if you want to succeed in any market you have to be good. Our friend the corporate caterer is good; she is bold, confident, and gives out an air of total competence. Her total assurance and professionalism quells any doubts her clients may have. Bad hair day, odd socks, grubby shoes, unreliability, and even a tiny hint of shiftiness and you are finished, dead in the water, caput! If you aren't ready to offer perfection that is consistent or even improving (yep, improving perfection), then wait a bit until you are sure you are ready. Second chances are hard to get.

POINTS TO PONDER ON 'REASSURANCE'

- You have a wonderful story to tell. If you can find a good way of telling it, it is a real winner but, most important, it secures your credibility and reassures the customer.

- Think about how you can reduce the perceived risk that your customers feel they are taking.

- It is no good just crashing about, hoping that you will bump into customers. You have to know who they are before you can find them.

- If we want corporate customers we have to realize that the buyer is taking a risk doing business with us and will need even more reassurance and a more believable, professionally-presented story.

- Bear in mind, unlike the individual who makes a buying mistake, the corporate buyer could get fired for doing business with you.

- We must be able to prove our competence, track record and history beyond all doubt to all customers but even more so with corporate customers.

- You have to be remarkable, outstanding and brilliant if you want to stand any chance at all of deposing the current supplier.

- Be aware of all the people involved in the decision making – all of them have to be kept happy – and be prepared to tailor your story to suit each one of them.

CHAPTER 16

WORKING THE ROOM

. . . In which we discover that you need to like people if you're in a people business, but whatever enterprise you are in you will have to learn to behave in a way that may not come naturally to you.

A GREAT BUSINESS . . . IF IT WASN'T FOR THE PEOPLE

The next area that baffles me is the personality of the self-employed person and the enterprises that they choose. Personalities build enterprises. If, to go back to an old chestnut, you open this mythical coffee shop, you will meet loads and loads of people. If you don't like people, what on earth are you doing opening a coffee shop?

We recently visited a local attraction which is a tiny model country with working trains, funfair, ships and buses. We took some very young relatives who were enchanted by it What wasn't enchanting at all were the proprietors! To look at them, you would think that this fairyland was their own private home and that, instead of paying a hefty whack to see it, you had broken in with the sole intent of befouling their treasured sanctuary. Not a smile or an acknowledgement, and a total rejection of any attempt to involve them in conversation, that is, until an elderly lady tried to photograph her grandchild's wide-eyed delight at the sight of the models. Then they pounced! "No photographs, can't you read?" they cried, pointing at a selection of threatening notices – one of which read 'No photographs'. Why no photographs? They offered no explanation. But that's not actually the point; if you hate and despise people that much and are so tired and exasperated by them, then why on earth would you involve yourself in a people enterprise? Take any rundown, ordinary, miserable little enterprise and do nothing else, nothing at all, other than smile, be nice, be welcoming, and be busily proactive and I guarantee income will quadruple.

THE MILITARY MAN

A retired military man came on one of my courses and, despite everything I did to dissuade him, he decided he wanted a country tea-shop. I visited his establishment a few months later; he had purchased, as described, a well established 'olde worlde tea shoppe' in a picturesque tourists' trap. It was a Sunday and the place was heaving, literally bursting at the seams with people. Our hero was rushing about like a blue-arsed fly. He spotted me and came straight across, his face red with exertion and emotion. He fixed me with a glare that seemed to suggest that I was at the heart of all his troubles. Choosing to ignore the signals I remarked breezily, "Seems to be going well?" Well that did it! He exploded there and then "Going well? Going well Look at this lot," he shouted, waving his arms in the general direction of the crowd who were not noticing this flailing shouting lunatic.

"Look at them gorging themselves on my food, befouling my bathrooms with their ghastly children, just coming and going when they feel like it and feeling they have the right to demand anything they want!" Taken aback by this tirade, I said, "Well, they are paying handsomely for the privilege – they pay your wages." "Pay my wages? No money on this earth should give trolls like this the right to order me about." At this he acquired a strange, high keening sort of whine which I was supposed to imagine was the collective voice of the general public. "Oooh, me tea's not 'ot. Squire, fetch me another slice of Battenberg. 'Av you got a bucket, me kid bin sick! I hate them all." At this he deflated like a balloon and trudged away to his fate.

PLAY NICE

I asked this earlier but I will ask you again: when you start your enterprise what job will you give yourself? Clearly, that guy should never have bought that tea shop. I tried to tell him that the job description 'Tea shop manager, whose duties are to include waiting on people, washroom cleanliness, and sorry, no weekends off' would not suit him. Even we normal human beings who have picked an enterprise that we will enjoy will find it getting tiresome or inconvenient once in a while.

My strange friend who does this odd bit of gardening admits he is not that fond of gardening, but he has a theory (albeit a bit weird) which is: at the heart of his life, on the whole he detests work and will avoid doing much of it whenever he can. He doesn't like working, it makes him depressed, but he has to do it to live. The theory then goes on to suggest that anything you have to do becomes work. So if you take his passion, which is riding his motorcycle, if he did that as a job – say dispatch riding, stunt show or motorcycle taxi, it would become work and rob him of his only pleasure. While I am not too sure about his thinking, I do see that even fun things which have to be done at a certain time, in a certain way, and at a certain place, can become demanding. But if you look at actors, for example, most of them got into that profession because of a passion for that art. They must get tired and depressed but if we had invested a large amount of money for tickets to see that long-running Broadway hit, we would be a bit miffed if, when the curtain went up, the star ambled to the front of the stage and said, "I am so bored with doing this. I've been stabbed in the final act 836 times and I'm tired of it." That never happens; every night we see a fresh dynamic show with breathtaking characters. For us it is the first time and the skill of the actors would never let us see that it was their 836th time. We need to do the same; we have to put on a show.

BEHAVIOUR MODIFICATION

During my research for my books, I enjoy delving into the world of interpersonal psychology. These psychologists have a flash name for finding ways to make people act differently. They call it 'behaviour modification'. One of the tenets of this practice is that 'behaviour changes behaviour', so, as long as we are aware, we can choose the behaviour that changes the subject's behaviour.

The tea shop owner, the family attraction owner, and my chum the gardener, may all be accused of having bad attitudes. Every chirpy self-help book wishes to improve our 'attitude' and for us it is a mystery as to why anyone would start a people-based enterprise if they had a bad attitude But hold up there a moment, what is an 'attitude'? The best definition I have ever heard is, 'Attitude is a behaviour that we choose for ourselves'. Eureka! That is the heart of this whole book; *Self Made Me* – we are not told any more, not forced, ordered, bossed, persuaded or enticed. No more the wage slave, no code of conduct for employees, no book of rules. Behaviour you choose for yourself; a life that you choose for yourself. So you've got a tea shop? You get up in the morning, look in the mirror and you see the tired dismal ageing thing looking back. What behaviour are you going to choose today? What part are you going to play? Why, the part of a cheery, welcoming, country tea shop owner, of course, the role that builds the business and makes money.

A biker at heart

In my heart and my lifestyle I am a fairly tatty looking biker, so imagine my wry smile when a critic described me as the 'archetypal business guru' looking at home and sharp in my Savile Row suit. I think I must be playing my part a bit too well but I made a horrible mistake once when travelling to a conference in some distant land. The suit, tailored shirts and silk ties were all nicely packed away in the luggage and I was travelling as 'me' in my battered and comfy leather jacket. The client met me at the airport and flipped! He really didn't want to let me present at the conference and it wasn't until he saw me in the monkey suit that he relented. Put on a show and then whip out of the stage door before your fans see you. If you have a small town enterprise you are on stage a lot longer than you may think. If you are Mr Tinkles the children's entertainer, don't start a huge punch up in the local bar in your spare time.

Strength of character

A good way to get your head around this is to write a tiny play where the star is a character who is a huge success in the enterprise you are planning. '"To the Stars"', a play by Geoff Burch. The principal character is Doris, a successful recruitment adviser.' Go on to describe the person's dress, activity levels, attitude and behaviour towards other people; how do they behave when they spot an opportunity; what other people think of them. Could you play that part? The thing is, if you can't then you are giving yourself the wrong job.

The right person for the job

In the preceding examples, some of the individuals mentioned should really never have gone into the 'people' business. Their natural inclination is to dislike interacting with people and I cannot understand why they would ever pick an enterprise that consisted of nothing but mixing with their fellow humans. The problem for us is that, even if we choose an enterprise that we might believe has limited interaction with others, we will always come up against behaviours that are required for success which may conflict with our natural inclinations. I would like this book to offer success to anyone who reads it, not just the extroverts but also to the shy and retiring. The fact is that the price we have to pay to become successfully self-employed is to occasionally work against our feelings and to be able to work outside our personal comfort zone.

If you look at professional entertainers, some of the most famous ones, who looked so smooth, casual and successful, were actually crippled by stagefright every single time and yet still managed to have a great career for many years. They believe that the stagefright is a price worth paying and, more importantly for us, despite it, they 'work the room'. You will have to learn to work the room – even if you make coffee tables and are shy you can't just hide away in your shed with your saw and plane and hope the public will beat a path to your door. So even if it is against your natural inclination and even if you have chosen a business you feel doesn't depend on human interaction, you are going to have to put on a show, put on a face, and get out there and grab those opportunities.

A GRINNING LUNATIC

I write a lot about customer care which involves a huge amount of smiling and so on, but this is so much more than that. Eager, friendly, smiley people still sometimes have 'loser' written all over them. Remember the amateur surgeon; he was friendly and chatty and still scared away potential customers. In the case of our friend the corporate caterer, she exudes confidence. If the potential client has any doubts before they meet her, they certainly don't afterwards. There is an American sales expert who, when he has a big deal to close, puts a hundred thousand dollars in cash in his jacket pocket. Just knowing it's there gets rid of any feelings of desperation he may have and he claims the deals close as if by magic.

WORKING FOR NOTHING

OK, where are we? We have chosen the correct enterprise, it will result in a job that we will enjoy doing day in and day out, we are competent and expert at the job, we understand and exceed our competitors big and small, and we know our potential customers and have tailored our offer precisely in a completely professional manner. So why haven't we got any work? Dare I say that it might be against our natural inclination and personality to suffer the perceived embarrassments and humiliations of going and talking to strangers, revealing personal information about ourselves, being forced to ask for money and risking being rejected. I cannot soften this blow – that is one of the downsides of self-employment and will always be with us. The only advice I can give is to remember that frightened but successful entertainer and just grit your teeth and get on with it. It does get easier, I promise.

If you remember my tirade about coffee table makers, taxi drivers, merchants and burglars, we looked at what the self-employed fool themselves into calling work. That poor old coffee table maker sweats away in their shed under the impression that, just because they are making hundreds of coffee tables, they are working. What they are in fact doing is expending effort for no reward, whilst I cheerfully claim that the correct definition of work is effort that someone (the customer or employer) is prepared to pay you for.

Well, perhaps I wasn't strictly honest with you there. Perhaps we ought to analyze the statement, 'Finding and keeping customers is the only activity that generates revenue; everything else involves us in cost'. Implicit in this statement is the fact that a lot of our effort will not be paid for – well, not directly.

Early on in this book I may have been a little harsh on employers. I suggested that if our employer pays us £20 an hour and sells the output of our effort for £100, then we are being paid a fifth of what we are worth. That employer has to find the work for us to do and when it is done they have to distribute it and get paid. As self-employed people we will be able to keep a much larger share of that pot – in other words, the profit, but we will have to bear the costs or consequences of the other side of the equation. We will have to do work that we don't appear to get paid for.

Finding work is work

Here is a nice bold statement of fact that you need to remember: 'Finding work, is work'. There are two things that the self-employed need to remember: finding work is work, and it is going to have to be paid for. It is no good saying, "I can afford to work for £20 an hour" if in a 40-hour week you spend 20 hours looking for work. This means that you will have to double your charges to cover the 'looking for work' time which, of course, makes work even harder to find.

You have covered the checklist; you are truly brilliant and ready to go. Now what? If you are crap, that is bad, but if you are not crap and have no work, that is worse. Even more dangerous are people who become self-employed because they have work lined up; maybe someone has a large project, or asked them to go freelance.

Cheesy

One of my least favourite books is *Who Moved My Cheese*, but it does have a simple core message that you would think would be obvious, but apparently not – so through gritted teeth I recommend that you read it. It suggests that if people (or mice, weirdly enough) find a place of plenty where the living is easy, they don't question the source or longevity of the situation. When the well, as it were, runs dry, they are shocked and bewildered.

If you have come to self-employment through redundancy, you may well have already experienced the feeling. Go to bed, get up, go to work, same old dreary job, same people, same jokes, same commute, same money, and then, "We're moving production to the Far East! Sorry. Bye bye." Don't tell me you really didn't see that coming? There will have been signs . . . meetings, closed rooms, strange measurements taken, unfamiliar faces about the place. Just don't make the same mistake now you are self-employed. Always be looking for the next piece of work or other opportunities.

When I am really busy I don't follow my own advice, so every feast is followed quite swiftly by a famine. I panic and throw myself into work-generating strategies, like PR, networking, blogging, writing articles and contacting my databases. Of course, this is all unpredictable slow-burn stuff so when the work starts to trickle back, it isn't long before I am hit by a tidal wave of work that overwhelms me. Well, as I said, the Buddhists say something like, "He teaches that which he needs to know most himself."

It's a steal

You may wonder at my choice of the burglar as my role model for self-employment. The overriding thing about this example is that the burglar has that rare and treasured ability to work wherever and whenever they want, and at a time and place of their own choosing. The other remarkable point about the burglar is that they are such consummate opportunists. Burglary is their core job description; yours may be cake maker, bar owner, lawyer, inventor or adviser, but in the case of the burglar there is an internal philosophical driver and that is dishonesty – a desire to steal anything that's not nailed down, to make money as quickly and as easily as possible, illegal or otherwise. The burglar may steal your wallet, sell pirate DVDs, grow illegal drugs, take a car to get home, or thieve an antique vase. The burglar's internal driver will not let him miss any opportunity for gain from dishonesty.

You have your job description but what is your driver, what will help you to spot your opportunities? Self-employment is not a job; it's a lifestyle – a way of life. When I see self-employment projects that fail when every aspect seemed to be in place to lead to success, the reason is so often missed opportunities. The frustrating thing is that it isn't as though the opportunities are hiding in some way. We see that wallet unguarded on the bar and (quite rightly) a set of moral codes and imperatives prevents us from taking it. We saw it, but we didn't steal it. The burglar would describe that as a missed opportunity. We have behaved well and honestly, our morals and our upbringing have prevented us from behaving dishonestly. The problem is that other elements of our upbringing, background and conditioning also prevent us from behaving effectively where it is legitimate and appropriate for our situation.

Seize the day

You overhear a conversation in a bar: "What I need is someone who can make my management team more effective". You stride across, hand over your card and brochure which you always carry with you, "I'm the person you are looking for! I have doubled the output of the following companies to which they will be delighted to attest. There is a newspaper article where I am described as the world's best management development expert. Now, when can I get started?" Brash, pushy, I bet the very idea is making you cringe with embarrassment, but that was your wallet on the bar, there for the taking. But those inner voices held you back, "Don't show off", "Don't be pushy", "Don't speak to strangers", "Don't risk getting rejected", "Being told no is an esteem-crushing blow", "Don't blow your own trumpet", and so on.

POINTS TO PONDER ON
'WORKING THE ROOM'

- Don't start a people enterprise if you don't like people.

- Just smiling and being nice can double your income.

- At the very least, with a bit of acting ability, you can play the part of somebody being nice.

- You can't have a day off from giving faultlessly brilliant and friendly service. Put on a show.

- Behaviour changes behaviour, so make sure you choose the right one.

- Write a play with you as the central character starring in the enterprise you have chosen. Then describe that character.

- Remember, finding work is work and will involve interacting with people and learning to behave in a way that may not come entirely naturally to you.

- Even when you are busy, continue looking for new work.

- Recognize an opportunity, and make the most of it even if doing so makes you feel uncomfortable.

CHAPTER 17

MARKETING – THE SEARCH FOR OPPORTUNITY

. . . In which we learn how marketing can only create opportunities; good marketing creates good opportunities and we learn how to make the most of them.

WHAT MARKETING WON'T DO

We are going to take a look at the thorny subject of marketing, but before we do we have to understand what marketing will and won't do for us. It does not sell; it does not find customers; it does not make money; it cannot find work. It does one very significant and valuable thing, it creates opportunities. For example, say you are a painter and decorator and you produce a few hundred cheap flyers which you drop in the mail boxes of all the surrounding homes in your neighbourhood. Miraculously, you get a phone call, someone would like their hall and stairs decorated, can you give a price. The first step is not to fool yourself into thinking that this is work coming in.

Great potential

During my start-up courses, a few weeks in there is always someone declaring that they have got loads of work. What they mean to say is loads of opportunities. That telephone call asking for a price or a quote means that you have been given the opportunity to go and secure that work. Sending out a quote and hoping for the best is way too hit and miss – and is mostly miss. The simplest and most scary solution is to go round to the POTENTIAL customers, sell yourself, sell your price, and then without a flicker or a bead of sweat, ask for the work. Again, I will say if you want to know how to do it, read some basic books on sales; the techniques are easy to master but implementation does need a bit of courage. More to the point, the leaflets were relatively costly (considering that we haven't earned any money yet), delivering them was a bind, and the response was a bit disappointing (it always is, we have a human tendency to pre-spend our lottery winnings after buying just one ticket).

Face to face is the only way

So now you have got this opportunity to quote, you get the job! Whoopee – but just hold on up there a moment, there must have been something that convinced our customer (not too cheap, I hope). Think about this, the front door could do with a lick of paint as could the dining room and the kitchen. The customer has a clear need, you want the work and they are convinced by you – so spot the opportunities and go for the rest of the work. The old "Look, while I am here, why don't I take a look at . . ." speech – opportunity leading to opportunity.

EXTRA! EXTRA! READ ALL ABOUT IT!

Let's talk about those good old coffee shops again. Look at your own town and the many coffee shops it will surely have. How is their marketing? I have already guessed your reply, "What marketing?" Expensive refit, fancy Italian steam driven coffee machines, dark wood chairs, leather sofas, a contemporary sign . . . so to just turn the sign to open and wait for the customers, unless your name is Starbucks, is a fatal strategy.

Let's look at the options: a big splash in the local press costing about £2000 and, amazingly, against every expectation the next morning you get a 10% response, that is 200 people in your coffee shop. Apart from being more people than you can possibly handle, they have cost you £10 each which is a great way to lose money fast.

Give the stuff away

OK, let's try this idea. We will go to bus stations, railway stations and crowded shopping areas, where we will hand out vouchers which cost virtually nothing to produce. The voucher entitles the bearer to a free cup of coffee. We can regulate the flow of people by the quantity of vouchers we hand out. It only costs us £1 and this is only when the voucher is redeemed. Two hundred customers only cost us £200 – a tenth of the cost of the press advertising. That means that at those costs we only go bust a tenth as slowly as the expensive alternative!

Up-sell

I won't compromise on my original statement – marketing only brings opportunity – but in this case, what is that opportunity? Stop here and really think about this question. How are you going to recover that £1 or, depending on your choice, that £10? The person comes in, hands over the voucher, gets their free coffee and then what?

You have two ways to seize that opportunity and you will need to do both. First, when the person has got the coffee you ask them to buy something: "A nice slice of homemade carrot cake? Go on, spoil yourself!"

Second, one of the best ways to recover your marketing investment is to secure repeat business. You can only do that if the experience for the customer is truly outstanding. There is no point inviting people to sample what your enterprise offers if what it offers is awful. By this I mean both service and product. You could go into the street, immaculately dressed, with the sunniest of sunny smiles, and offer people dog poo on little slices of Melba toast. They might even smile at you and say "delicious" but I can assure you it is not an experience they would willingly repeat. My absolute obsession is the idea of customer loyalty which is a very fragile treasure indeed – and I would like to introduce a little bit of paranoia in you by suggesting that at your first slip in quality, appearance or service, there will be somebody waiting to take your customer away from you. It is also important to note that it is not what *we* call good, it is what the *customer* calls good.

The legend of the pickled onion

I had a friend who decided that he had finished with the cut and thrust of city life, and with his ill-gotten gains he purchased a large fish and chip shop. He challenged me to think of a sales tip that would help the fish and chip business. We told his team that every time they started to wrap the hot food, they should smile and say, "Shall I pop in a pickled onion?" Insignificant? At the end of the first year they had sold £15,000 worth of pickled onions.

Coffee shops and fish and chip shops are just working examples to make a simple point. No matter what you want to do, whenever you find yourself in front of a customer there is an opportunity for you to ask them to buy something.

GIFT OF THE GAB

Someone was listening to me once and said, "It's alright for you!" I asked him what he meant. "Well I mean . . . you've got the gift of the gab, you silver-tongued deceiver! If I could master that I would never look back." "OK," I said, "I'm yours! What would you like me to do for you?" "Them!" he cried, pointing out of the window at a glittering skyscraper. "I want an appointment with them." It turns out that this guy had recently started an office cleaning enterprise and saw this tower block as nirvana. The problem was that every attempt to contact them was rebuffed. Strangely enough, I happened to know the Chief Executive. "I know the boss! Would you like an appointment with him?" The answer was eager and affirmative.

"Hello, Consolidated Reinsurance, how may I help you?"

"Yes, good morning, could you put me through to Sir Charles please?"

"Who is calling, please?"

"Tell him it's his old pal Geoff!"

"Geoff! My old friend! Great to hear from you, how can I help you?"

"I've got a chum who has an office cleaning business. He would love a few minutes of your time."

"Anything for you, Geoff. When can he come?"

"Would tomorrow afternoon be OK, around 3.00 pm?"

The next day there is a knock on Sir Charles' door. "Come! Enter our friend, gripping his flat hat. "Ah, you must be Geoff's friend. Take a seat and tell me all about yourself."

"That's very kind of you, your honour; well I have just started office cleaning . . ."

"Is it going well?"

"Not bad!"

"Good, good, and do you have a brochure?"

"Yes, your mightiness. I've got these – my brother designed them when he was in prison as part of his anger management programme."

"Such vivid colours! Well, it's been wonderful to meet you and I hope you have every success."

"Thank you so much, your lordship, you've been very kind."

He met me with a look of excitement in his eyes. "How did it go?," I asked.

"Brilliant! He was so nice and friendly."

"So you asked him for the work, the cleaning contract for that building?"

"Well, I didn't like to, he was so nice I didn't want to upset him, he would have only said 'no'."

That's when I blew! "No, is where the selling starts. I have called in a once in a lifetime favour, got you an unrepeatable appointment and you have wasted it."

OPENING DOORS

For the new enterprise there are a few points to consider in that story. Firstly, the job I actually did was a marketing one; the opening of doors and appointment getting is all marketing. Some people talk about telephone selling or tele-sales, but just pause and think, if your enterprise is a complicated, new or expensive one, there is no way you can sell it on the phone. Understand that when I say 'sell', I mean done, dusted and money handed over. What you can do with the phone, as with all marketing, is to create opportunities.

Just a ring

How many times have you been called by a nice, genuine person who says, "We have just taken over a country pub. We think we do the best Sunday lunches in the world and we would love to invite you to come and try us out. To tempt you, we are offering our delicious traditional puddings free with every lunch." Not very often, I bet! For the new enterprise this tele-marketing (as it should be called) is a gritty, tough business but it does create opportunities.

Remember the coffee bar and those vouchers; the first way to make money is to sell something, the second way to recover the cost, both financial and emotional, is to secure repeat business. I mean, those Sunday lunches better be the best in the world, and maybe it was a good thing our office cleaner didn't get the job because he may not have been ready to give a brilliant, remarkable and efficient service. The coffee shops I have been to with bad coffee, thick cups and stale cakes – why should I go back?

BEWARE AWARE

There is a big thing in marketing called brand awareness – that means getting people to know about you. Well, if you are crap we do not want to make people aware of that. If you were that office cleaner, how would you handle that situation? First look at your target customer. Are you absolutely get-set ready to exceed the expectations that your marketing generated? If you are, when you get those opportunities, are you making the most of them by securing the business and then asking for more? Do you have a budget for marketing and, if you do, are you aware how you will recover those costs time and time again?

A bit of a headache

While marketing creates opportunities it does another vital thing and that is it creates expectations. The danger is they are expectations that are both intentional and unintentional. If I see you munching an aspirin I may be tempted to ask you why.

"Headache, Geoff, terrible headache."

"I'm sorry, what have aspirins got to do with a headache?"

"I've taken them before."

"Ah . . . previous experience, satisfied customer, repeat business."

"No, I think my mum told me about them."

"Ah, third party recommendation!"

"No, I know I saw an advert in the paper. It said, EAT ASPIRIN, CURE HEADACHE!"

Great marketing, that! A simple message that creates expectations. That phone call we received creates expectations of the world's greatest Sunday lunch, but the leaflet designed in an anger management class produces the unexpected expectation of an unprofessional klutz.

Give a dog a bad name

So here is the message: all of our marketing must be sharp, professional, well designed and well considered. We do not want our target customers to look at our Day-Glo stars, floppy business cards and computer-generated leaflets and think 'loser'! When you are marketing, don't hold back, let rip with the 'finely crafted', 'lovingly produced', 'considered the most delicious', 'a fabulous investment', but . . . and this is a huge but . . . these are expectation promises. You now have to deliver finely crafted, lovingly produced, delicious, fabulous investments. Customer loyalty – the backbone of successful self-employment – depends on us delivering all our promises.

POINTS TO PONDER ON 'MARKETING – THE SEARCH FOR OPPORTUNITY'

- All marketing can do for you is to create opportunities. It is up to you what you do with them.

- Marketing, big or small, will always involve you in costs and you must realize that cost has to be recovered.

- A potential customer is a rare treasure. Don't forget to make money out of them by selling them something and then delight and thrill them so much that they will want to come back again and again.

- Because of the cost of marketing, don't market yourself until you are ready to delight. You don't want to spend money showing people how bad you can be.

- However you get these opportunities, don't waste them – you may not get a second chance.

- Customer loyalty depends on what the customer judges to be good, not what you call good.

- Marketing also creates expectations – are you ready to fulfill them?

- Badly produced marketing produces an expectation of a badly produced enterprise.

CHAPTER 18

WEB OF INTRIGUE

. . . In which we discover how we can harness the fearsome power of the World Wide Web for our own profit and advancement.

THE WORLD IS YOUR VIRTUAL OYSTER

The elephant in the room and the thing that has transformed my enterprise for good and ill is that good old World Wide Web. It means that everyone can have a global presence and it also means that traditional employment is even more pointless.

To repeat the point made earlier, if your job can be done at the other end of a wire, it is probably under threat. On the other hand, if you are self-employed, you may well be able to do your job at the other end of a wire. If you analyze aerial photography for forensic examination, you can have clients from Kathmandu to Bogota. If you teach a foreign language you can do it over the Skype network to anywhere in the world. So it still escapes me why employers should want to lock hundreds of bored, listless people up at great expense in a large concrete and glass structure just to keep an eye on them. Even more weirdly, why would you let yourself be locked up there just for some non-existent job security?

It could be suggested that it is our obsession with process, the traditional manager's fixation – not with 'what have you achieved?' but with the 'how did you achieve this?'. If you are an ex-manager and can let go of this illness of overmanaging the process, you can, with the help of global connectivity, become a world wide multibillion dollar mega corporation from your back bedroom.

To take this idea to its most ludicrous conclusion you could commission a number of freelance vehicle designers to design a range of family-sized cars, you could email the designs to manufacturers in the Far East, appoint independent garages as distributors and bingo, you are a volume car manufacturer from the third bedroom of 'Bide-a-wee', 47 Dingle Avenue, Anytown.

A lot of fish in this sea

The danger of the internet is that it is like a great big magnifying glass. It can magnify our opportunities but it can also focus on any element of crappiness and magnify that just as easily. First and foremost, here is a bold statement: YOU DO NEED A WEBSITE.

I have a very dear friend who is a brilliant technician in a certain field – in truth, he is probably the best in the world but, despite constant nagging, he just will not have a website. There is no doubt whatsoever that his work is in constant decline to the point that he is finding money short, and he says in a wonderfully mournful way, "How can I spend money on a website when I need to eat?" My reply? "No website, no eat!"

My own website, which I am never totally settled with, brings in work from all over the world. To my friend the technician, it's like looking into a bucket devoid of fish when there is an ocean full of them behind him that he could drop his line into. If your enterprise is a traditional one, say, house painting, child care, gardening or catering, not having a website is like not having a postal address or a telephone number.

Net the opportunities

At the other end of the spectrum there are web-based enterprises that only exist in cyberspace and then there are the enterprises, like my own, that become a success because they are transitional. In other words, they were started traditionally but have discovered new opportunities on the internet.

An accountant, laid off from a large corporation, started, as one would, to work as an independent accountant for small firms. For some reason his website hit the mark and scores of small firms from all over the place started to contact him. What now? Expansion? Employees? Apart from good presentation, efficiency, and general pleasantries, his key attraction was cost effectiveness (oh, OK, he was cheap!). Any expansion could compromise this so he discovered that the miracle of the internet meant he could get the grunt work of the audit done by very skilful people in Bangalore, India. While my car manufacturer fantasy is a joke, this guy's international accountancy practice isn't.

WHAT CAN THE WEB DO FOR US?

To get this techno-adventure under way, we need to decide what it is we want the web to do for us. As a marketing tool, it produces more opportunities, but remember, they are just opportunities. But the web can actually sell and bring in money, so is it a shop we are building here? It is also our showcase for the world to have a look at us and what we do. The potential customers can speak to other customers who love us, they can sample our work, see us in action, and they can contact us.

I am absolutely paranoid about my website. Is it any good; where does the professionalism of its construction rank me with the other sites you have visited? When you build a site with your biography, pictures, video clips and testimonials, you are literally exposing yourself or your products to scrutiny and comparison. The cheapest way into this is to design and build your own site – a number of the hosting companies and internet providers offer free or cheap website design. I don't know what advice to offer because you may be very talented at web design, I just know that I am not. It is like saying that because you can hold a coloured pencil, you are capable of designing your logos, adverts and publicity material. In my case, I feel it necessary to hire in some professional help. I have a truly brilliant genius who I refer to as my techno-troll, but just because he is a genius doesn't mean that he and I don't have very heated and controversial arguments about the purpose of a website.

OPTIMIZE DON'T COMPROMISE

If you talk to a skilful website builder there are certain obsessions that they have, and from my observations one of those is website optimization. If you already have a website I bet you have been hassled by companies offering to optimize your site. There are websites where you can measure the ranking in global terms of your site. The technicalities of this are hugely complex and involve loads of techno-troll speak about Bots and spiders. I have no technical know-how about this whatsoever, so let me explain my understanding of this and how it will impact on us.

Search engines such as Google look for things on the internet when we ask them to. We, the consumers, are Google's real customers and it does its best to find what we are looking for. If we type in 'window cleaner' it will try and find one for us. If our enterprise should happen to be window cleaning we, of course, would like to be found. The search engine has a look at the World Wide Web and sees millions of window cleaners. The problem is that when the search results appear, the consumer only really picks from the first one or two pages of choices. The search engine has all sorts of weird and esoteric ways of favouring one site over another – at one time, it was key words like 'cheapest', 'Elvis Presley', or 'pole dancing'. The trick was to type them over and over again, black on black, so the viewer couldn't see them, but the search engine could. Of course, Google rumbled that stunt and started disqualifying some sites.

Popularity then became important; the answer was to get Far Eastern call centres to hit and hit and hit on your site. Then links to prestige sites like Fox News or the BBC were important. As Google got tougher, the techno-trolls got more slippery. To the trolls, the measure of success was the amount of traffic (or visitors to the site).

Nearly famous

My personal techno-troll is absolutely brilliant at this; he capers about calling out that I have a diddly pom or doo-hickey rating of eight hundred thousand! "Is that good?" I ask. "Oh yes," he cries, "last year you were four million." This means that on one scale or another I am, in the business world, the eight hundred thousandth most famous person. To me, when you consider all the stars and galaxies, to be eight hundred thousandth on this little spinning ball of mud seems a little insignificant but my troll assures me that it's brilliant!

Now, this is the important bit: I don't seem to feel any richer. The scoring is based on the number of visitors to the site. To this end we tried to construct a site that was entertaining, amusing and informative. The result has been what I call "masturbating teenagers" My trolls get really angry with me when I start that but my explanation is that while the site may attract millions of cheery visitors, how do I get any money out of them?

All the fun of the fair

Another downside of this is that if people have enjoyed your site you can end up in the funfair trap.

There is a business model that offers a funfair or a carnival as the perfect business structure. Why do you visit a funfair? Because you have been before and know that it's fun. What disappoints you when you get there? When everything's the same and there are no new rides, or when everything is different and your favourite ride is not there. So they have to be as expected, but always have something new and exciting to see. Oh, and they have to suit all tastes with kiddy rides in the day and white-knuckle at midnight. If I am busy, tired or unconscious for a while and neglect my blog or video clips, I get a storm of emails complaining – or worse, a decline in visitor numbers.

WEIRD AND WONDERFUL

Let's, for our little trip together, forget the technical stuff and see where the web helps us on our journey. First, why do people visit websites? For me, I visit for things that are cheap, weird or specific. For 'cheap', for example, my typical specific Google will be 'flights to Hong Kong' – the results will help me to pick the cheapest of the least dangerous airlines; I will be offered compromises of airport, timing and price; I make my choice and buy. In the 'weird' category I look for unusual steam engines for sale or collectable pinball machines, and for the 'specific', I mighty type in a person's name or a particular part number.

My name is Geoff Burch and, strangely enough, the name of my website is Geoff Burch. Guess what, if you want to find me you should type in 'Geoff Burch'. Forgetting any Bots and spiders, the result happens to come back with websites with Geoff Burch in their title.

If you run the 'Cheering Lizard' reptile shop, then if someone types in 'cheering lizard' they will find you. Where things become hard work is when someone types in 'Business author self-employment' – I don't think I would be found. Or if you type, 'I want a gecko', the 'Cheering Lizard' might not appear. You would have to work really hard to get those more oblique requests to find you and one has to judge whether that is worthwhile. In other words, consider coming at this backwards. If people know who you are they will Google you by specific name and find you.

Remember, I am doing well as eight hundred thousandth; it is just that I wonder whether people who have a bundle of cash in their hand will fight through the other seven hundred and ninety nine thousand, nine hundred and ninety nine to get to me!

A load of balls

When the visitors do get to you, what offer are you going to make to them and how easy is it to work your site? The other question is: are you going to have a web-based enterprise?

Let me run a simple thought by you. Let's imagine that I would like to sell golf balls. I cannot think of a better web-based business. I have a source of brand name golf balls at ridiculously low prices. After a great deal of thought, I have decided to call this site 'Cheap Golf Balls'. The reason is that the parsimonious golfer will type into Google, 'cheap golf balls' and if you do sell cheap golf balls you are in business . . . well, as long as they are around the cheapest golf balls in the world. The site will be easy, too; no music, no dancing girls, no hilarious cartoons or chatty blogs, there will be a picture of a golf ball or a box of golf balls, a list of prices and a 'buy now' button. If you don't like people or want to live dressed only in skin-tight latex you can sit in a shed somewhere dispatching millions of golf balls and becoming rich. Here endeth the business plan.

Let's be twee

If you have got to here by reading this book so far, you will have noticed that I hate and deride twee names. That also got tipped on its head by the internet.

As you know, I suggest that if your name is Susan West and you ice cakes, you would be well advised to call the enterprise 'Susan West Design' and not something like 'Ends in Tiers'. The search engines would struggle with either of those but if it was called the 'Iced Cake Company' you may well get found. So, possibly a twee name is a good idea if it describes exactly what your enterprise is about, i.e. The Window Cleaning Company, Cheap Golf Balls,

Wedding Gifts, or Rent-a-Car. I know they're not exactly twee but I hope you can see what I mean.

WORDS ARE CHEAP

It is also worth contemplating here what we could sell on the internet. If one of the things the consumer looks for is value for money, whilst it may be difficult to find golf balls that are cheap enough for us to make a margin, not to put too fine a point on it, the contents of our head are very cheap indeed.

If we know a jolly amusing little song and can sing it reasonably well, people may well pay us a dollar to download it to their MP3 players – cost of production, nil, cost of storage (in your head), nil, received, one dollar, profit, one dollar. While Machiavelli said, "Knowledge is power", Geoff Burch says, "Knowledge is cheap" (but, of course, can be very valuable). By that I mean, to us, the suppliers of the knowledge, it's cheap, but to our customers it can be extremely valuable and worth paying for. For example, if you grew up and live in a Spanish-speaking country, that is a no-cost consequence of birth, but because I would like to improve my Spanish I would pay good money to have Skype conversations with you. If you train, and then hold webinars or offer subscription downloads, whether that is easy to sell or not is beside the point, the thing is that the manufacturing cost is zero.

Don't take my word for it
This leads us to a dodgy, or possibly illegal, area so the usual caveats, reservations and warnings apply here. Another cheap thing to sell is something you haven't got. I picked a hint of this up from Timothy Ferriss's *The Four Hour Work Week* (a recommended read on the whole cyber-business thing). The point is that self-employed people who set up a new enterprise tend to throw themselves into it with fearsome gusto, only to crash and burn in spectacular style. They believe they have a great idea and then they

bet the farm on it. To take that analogy a little further, when the tornado has passed, they are left with one small goat, a pile of wreckage and a heap of debt, but let us consider the cyber world for a moment.

In the real world you may decide to open a shop, 'The Hilarious Knitted Vegetable Cover Emporium'. What a cracking idea, you chuckle, in front of your log fire, sipping an amusing little claret while congratulating yourself on the elegance of your plan. The problem is that you will have to lease a shop.

> Can we stop here for a tirade? It was just that word 'lease' gave me such a shiver that I had an 'I can see my own breath' moment as when the undead stroll into the room! People with huge amounts of money (like banks and landlords) like to hang on to it, and when they invest for a return they like to know that it will return for a long time. Simple formula: you sign lease, they grow rich, you grow poor for a long time. Leases on premises can run for 25 years so you can be personally liable for 25 years. Even if the project is successful you will want flexibility of premises. At the time of writing, the commercial property market is in crisis and there are empty shops and units everywhere. So if you have to have premises, get a bit tough; no lease, short lease, or walk away. Think about millstones and necks!

Back to the Cyber Shop. You will have to fill your shop with stock and wait. What do people do when they walk into shops? They pick things up, they look at them, they check the price, you may engage them in conversation, they may or may not buy, and they amble out again.

Can we examine the risks? First, of course, there is the chance that no one buys anything; next, there may not be enough people buying anything – perhaps because of the location there are not enough people or the wrong sort of people are visiting. If your hilarious vegetable covers don't sell, you are done – another 24 years and 6 months of rent to pay, four tons of unsold vegetable covers, and a whole pile of worry.

In the cyber world all of these troubles just melt away. I have a place on my site that my techno-troll is very, very excited about. It is a bit he called my shop. You can visit my shop and buy things, mostly books, but there are DVDs, eBooks, tee-shirts, and even me (you can buy 'me' for your conference). The reason he is excited is because he designed it and thinks it is a very good shop as it is bulging with clever technical wizardry. My feeling is that, although it does well, it maybe doesn't work quite as well as the old shop.

The fact is, this whole thing is an illusion. It is not a shop, it is a picture of a shop. When you pick up a book and flick through a few pages, you are pressing a button to look at pictures of a few pages of a book that may, or may not, exist. Perhaps there are no books there at all, maybe I have never written a book in my life – and I never will unless enough people order one. Hang on, you are reading this, but this may be a sample page and if you are enjoying it I might write the rest. Can you see where I am coming from?

The case of the woolly carrot

You can test run websites and online shops: instead of having crap business ideas that cost you every penny you possess, you can now have virtual crap business ideas that don't cost a penny. 'The Hilarious Knitted Vegetable Cover Emporium' can be launched in cyberspace to see how it goes. The advantages are that you don't really need any stock to get started, the whole world is your footfall (however stupid the idea, in this entire world somebody may well be stupid enough to want a knitted vegetable cover or wish to teach their dog to weld), and you can keep trying different things. You could create many websites, 'Woolly Veg R Us', 'Cover Your Legume', 'Knit before Boiling', or go for the niches with 'Hide Your

Carrot', 'Insulate Your Aubergine'. The tiniest changes make a difference.

I came across someone who wanted to sell beautiful handmade shoes on the internet, but to do that would have required an enormous investment in lasts, leather and a knowledge of the most popular sizes. So what he did was to offer the shoes for sale before he had any stock of them at all. I'm not sure how legal or moral that activity was but what did happen was that he received a large number of orders for a very specific range of sizes and colours that showed him the way forward. Of course he refunded the money, but what it did tell him was that the business was viable, only certain colours were popular, and that the demand fell into a very narrow range of sizes. When the site was launched for real he knew he was going to make sales, he knew which stock was going to be popular, and had a list of people who had already stated their interest in his potential product.

If we set up something like that and the response to our offer is disappointing, we should email back and say that we regret that the offer was sold out and unfortunately we can get no further stock – all money fully refunded, of course. If the response is good, the reply would be, "We have been overwhelmed by the response to this offer and are now out of stock. Would you like a full refund or are you able to wait 28 days for our new stock to arrive?"

As a professional speaker, I get a lot of my work from speaking agencies which come and go, but one in particular gave us a lot of work. Whenever I searched for my name there were a number of speaking agencies in different fields of expertise that featured me, but I didn't recall ever doing business with them. As I am sure you have already guessed, they were all the same guy who was not so much an agent as a cyber-expert who knew how to manipulate the search engines. The thing for us to consider is that the one thing that made him different from vegetable covers or welding dogs was that he could stock or obtain known products – namely me! Type in stuff you want – Geoff Burch; Sony TV; VW spares – those are things widely looked for by name. You just have to convince the search engines that you are the best, the cheapest, the most used, or the handiest person to do that.

HANDYMAN

Of course there will be recognized services that will be searched for: Thai massage, plumbers or car hire. Even if you can't manipulate search engines and you offer a service, you had better have a smart, professional website. You will be found and some search criteria are geographical, so me typing 'plumber' may well result in me getting the nearest one to me. That could be you!

Then people search for knowledge bases: 'Can I sell more?', 'Fix a Chevrolet gearbox' or, one in my own case was, 'how can I weld aluminium with a mig welder?' (Don't ask.) On that one we got a great free film clip which was brilliant. We could have been charged for that but the maker of the clip instead used it to promote their great welding kit, which takes us neatly on to social media.

SHIPS THAT PASS IN THE NIGHT

A brilliant feature of the internet is how it broadens our horizons. You will remember in the story of the burglar how he benefited from forming loose alliances for specific jobs. For the self-employed, these sorts of opportunities are magnified by the internet and we can form alliances and contacts with people all over the world. I received an email a while back from someone in Singapore who wanted me to collaborate with them on a book they were written. We had no conversations or contact other than by email and yet we successfully completed the task which resulted in a book that had been specially written for the Far Eastern market. It also gives us the opportunity, as self-employed people, to outsource some of our tasks. Where previously we may have needed the services of a very expensive professional such as a tele-marketer, lawyer or designer, if we search the globe we can find these services at a fraction of the price we would pay locally.

Another thing we can do is to find support and reward by collaborating with our fellow professionals and by using professional contact sites such as LinkedIn where we can be in contact with other professionals who can share and introduce us to valuable work. Whilst writing this, I have realized how much of my contact is done through email and how many of my customers come to me through the internet, and because of that how my horizons have been expanded. I have travelled around the world from Kuala Lumpur to central Mexico and the only reason is because people have found me on the internet. A few years ago, those opportunities would not have been open to me. The world literally is your oyster.

ALL OF A TWITTER

First question, why? My publishers and publicists are very keen to get me involved in Facebook, Twitter, blogging and YouTube, but in my opinion we could be back into masturbating teenager territory. I would love to promote successful 'self made me's', but would having 20,000 followers on Twitter do that? I do put practical tips on YouTube and I do blog when I have the time. The difficulty is that if you become popular and stop, it really upsets people. What I am saying is, use these things as tools but be aware of your target audience, your target customer, commitment, and the image you would like to create. It is very difficult to uncreate an image out there. The pay-off is that, if you create a name, you will be searched for by name. If you can knit a vegetable cover while wing walking or assaulting a celebrity in an amusing way, it will be a YouTube hit and many people will search the internet for you. When friends visit each other, someone will casually pick up a Fairisle clad parsnip and say, "Ah, one of these things! Have you seen the clip on YouTube?"

MEET YOURSELF COMING BACK

A tip I give to all self-employed people is to visit yourself. If you have a shop, stand the other side of the street and look at it as a customer would; phone your office and try to do business with yourself. The key . . . and a real clincher, is, are you easy to do business with? This is never truer than in cyberspace. Visit your own site – is it easy to find, does it look great, professional and slick? When a specific order is placed, is the product easy to find, size and price? Is it easy to pay? (We use PayPal as it proved easier than the hoo hah the credit card companies put you through).

Just the same mistakes are made on the internet as they are in real life; the business expert who thinks it's cool and on the ball to wear a Winnie the Pooh tie is dead in the water. The website that blares out with jolly music and a rib-tickling animation is just as dead. Think about this . . . a lot of people who have the misfortune of still being employed in a 'proper' job will spend most of their time sneaking around the internet looking for stuff, so a fanfare of loud music and a brightly coloured flickering screen is the last thing they want when the boss is about.

Reducing the risks

The web is like a huge magnifying glass and it magnifies everything that we do. It can amplify the number of customers we can connect with, it can amplify the quantity of contacts we can make, but the downside of this is that it can also amplify our crappiness and amplify the perceived risk that our customers take by doing business with us.

Can you remember the formula that our customers use when looking for us? They want maximum benefit and minimum risk. With all of the scams, fiddles and rip-offs that exist in cyberspace, people are even more cautious when doing business on the internet and if you want your enterprise to succeed we have to find sure-fire ways of reassuring our potential customers.

Consider your own buying habits on the internet when choosing, say, a holiday. What's the first thing that you look for? For many people, it is independent reviews, so every time you do a good job make sure you get a good testimonial and ensure that it's one of the first things your potential customers see on your website. If you are getting a 100% customer satisfaction, tell the world, it helps to reassure. Offer plenty of guarantees – although this is a risky thought don't just offer money back but offer more than money back, i.e., "If you are not delighted with our golf balls, we will refund double your initial outlay."

A thing that we did before PayPal came along was that we sent ordered books out with no payment and allowed the customer to pay when they arrived. Strangely enough, I don't think we ever got let down – except by a large international corporation, would you believe! If people feel they are being trusted, they feel a sense of commitment.

When it comes to payment you can use a system like PayPal or any other secure payment system, so that the customer knows their money is safe until they are delighted with whatever they receive.

The final big reassurance, which is something that is unique to the self-employed individual, can be the human touch. If there is a strange query or if things go wrong, be prepared to be on the end of a telephone or send a personal email that shows in this big spooky cyberworld there is a kind, thoughtful human being involved who can sort things out personally.

To sum up, the internet is a great place to test business ideas. The world can be your customer, niches become less niche – i.e. when millions are viewing you. Everyone has to have a professional website – it's the world's window on you.

POINTS TO PONDER ON
'WEB OF INTRIGUE'

- You must have a website.

- If your job can't be done at the end of a wire, it might be safe from the internet threat.

- If your job can be done at the end of a wire, you can be doing your job anywhere in the world for anyone in the world.

- Before plunging in, have a clear idea of what you would like the web to do for you and your enterprise.

- Good website design is important because it is your window on the world.

- Whilst knowledge is a valuable resource, it can be very cheap to store and reproduce for your customers on the internet.

- Think about setting up trial sites, trial offers, and even trial stock, so that you can test the waters before you put any real money into it.

- Use the internet to develop useful liaisons and contacts.

- You can use social media to become web-famous – just make sure it is famous for being brilliant.

- Visit and work your own website regularly. Judge the customer experience and look for constant improvement.

- People feel that they are taking a risk doing business on the web, so try to make every effort to reduce that perceived risk in order to succeed.

CONCLUSION

Well, there we have it, the end of our short time together. I hope that this book has inspired you to do something – hopefully, to become successfully self-employed. If, on the other hand, it has put you off for now, perhaps that's no bad thing either, because taking the step that leads you into employing yourself can be a momentous one. It is literally life-changing and if you can make a success of it you will, I assure you, never want a 'proper job' again.

You may think that at times my messages have been tough, but most of the failures I have seen in self-employment have been because of simple mistakes and unrealistic expectations. If I have alerted you to the pitfalls, hopefully you won't fall into them.

This book has been a very different one for me to write; my other books have been written by me with a great deal of sweat and effort, but they are about what I know. This book is different because it is about how I feel, who I am, and how I live. Just like the burglar burgles, as a guru I go guru-ing, as it were, but my motivation, my internal machine, is that of a free self-employed person.

I sell what I do – that's where my customers get value, I don't sell who I am. The people who pay me don't possess me. I have been self-employed for most of my life although I have been tempted into proper jobs which all ended in dismal misery on every side.

I was going to make a very dangerous statement which everybody counselled me against, so I will make it but with an explanation that should, hopefully, get me off the hook. Here goes: 'Employment is for losers.' Now here is the explanation. I am not suggesting that if you have a proper job you are a loser, but you are losing so many things, some of which are: you are losing by not seeing your kids grow up; you are losing by not resting when the job in hand is finished; you are losing by not being able to do a day's work dressed only in your underwear or on a tropical beach; you are losing by not being paid what you are worth; and you are losing by not achieving your true value.

The proper job is a construct of the 19th and 20th centuries, a time when we had to be tied to the machine. Before that people thrived, prospered, and grew self-worth and respect from their self-employed pursuits. If you look at a mediaeval town, the various self-employed skills became the family names which are still with us today. Think about it: Farmer, Goldsmith, Baker, Miller, Fletcher (makes arrows), Bowman, Tanner and Weaver – all proud surnames that came from a time when the individual could grow and be proud of what they did with no boss, no appraisals, and no nine to five.

The fascination for me while writing this is how some succeed and some fail. Some stagger by and others become rich and famous, all for doing more or less the same thing. I meet a person who has failed in a catering enterprise one day and then the next day I am talking to a celebrity chef. What separates them? Is it talent? The answer must be that if you can learn that talent then you must, and if you can't learn it then stay away from catering, but I believe it has rarely got anything to do with talent. I have heard beggars at railway stations who play guitar as well as any rock star I have ever heard, so no lack of talent there then. Is it lucky breaks? Sure, it can be, but it is funny that the people who work the hardest at it seem to get the best luck.

My wife and I work very closely together and she can be my harshest critic (remember how useful honesty can be), so as we started to wrap this book up my paranoia set in and I asked her to reassure me as to what sort of book it was. She thought for a while and said, "I suppose it is a sort of buddy book based on the observations, mistakes, cock-ups and victories that you have had during your long relationship with self-employment."

Well, perhaps that's what it is. Whilst I would love you to take on board what I say, remember, I am not your boss, I'm your buddy. This book is based on my mistakes in self-employment, my observations on self-employment, and my personal experiences of self-employment. It is not a book of instructions from on high, it is your buddy, your coach just adding and contributing to your thoughts. Maybe this should be the first lesson – you will not, from this day forward, be told what to do any more, no more commands or orders – stupid or otherwise – no memos or emails of demand. You will, as you do with this book, have to consider the evidence and make your own decisions. Can you live with that? A lot of people can't and find it too scary.

Self-employment is a great game and one that you can win but, like all games, it has to be played by the rules. Maybe this 'buddy book' can help you a bit with those rules by giving tips and hints that will help you to avoid trouble. I suppose my qualification for doing that is because I've been in a whole heap of trouble quite a few times myself, so just like the burglar, when you get locked up with me, the old lag, let me share with you the best ways of avoiding trouble. As you take this rollercoaster ride of ups and downs, I will be your buddy.

The excuses, "It just didn't work out" or "I couldn't find the work" just won't wash any more. In this world of outplacement, relocation to the Far East, and outsourcing, our employers can no longer be relied on to keep us in employment. Self-employment is the only safe employment. Put trust in yourself – self-employment is the only place you will achieve true self worth and receive your true personal value.

BIBLIOGRAPHY

Magnus Lindkvist, *Everything we Know is Wrong: The Trend Spotters Handbook*, Marshall Cavendish, 2011.

Robert H. Waterman and Tom Peters, *In Pursuit of Excellence: Lessons from America's Best-Run Companies*, Profile Books, 2004.

Robert M. Pirsig and Michael Kramer, *Zen and the Art of Motorcycle Maintenance: An Inquiry into Values*, Vintage Classics, 2008.

Matthew Crawford, *The Case for Working With your Hands: Or Why Office Work is Bad for Us and Fixing Things Feels Good*, Penguin, 2010.

Matthew Crawford, *Shop Class as Soulcraft: An Inquiry into the Value of Work*, Penguin Books, 2010.

Timothy Ferriss, *The 4-Hour Work Week: Escape the 9–5, Live Anywhere and Join the New Rich*, Vermilion, 2011.

Ricardo Semler, *Maverick! The Success Story Behind the World's Most Unusual Workplace*, Random House, 2001.

Spencer Johnson, *Who Moved my Cheese: An Amazing Way to Deal with Change in Your Work and in Your Life*, Vermilion, 1999.

ACKNOWLEDGEMENTS

Grateful thanks to my tireless and hardworking missus, Sallie, who sweated blood to help build this book; and to Holly, Iain, Megan and all the rest of the Capstone team for attempting to keep me on the straight and narrow.